# A Walk Through Wissett

*Mill House windmill reconstructed.*

*The Rogation walk through Wissett c1970, including, from the front – Andrew Macfarlane, Stephen Oddy, Jeanie Macfarlane, Maureen Hunt and Teresa Wing, Sally Reeder and Sadie Wing, Micheline Talbot, Emma and Mrs Joel, Deborah Kiddy and Mrs Lifton.*

# A Walk Through Wissett

edited by

## Diana Fernando
and
## Helen Flaxman

First Published 2001
Copyright    © 2001 Helen Flaxman and Diana Fernando
ISBN         1-902626-44-3

Published by    Red Bird Publishing Ltd
                Colchester, Essex CO7 0SX

Printed by      Technographic Design & Print Ltd
                Colchester, Essex CO7 0SX and
                Halesworth, Suffolk IP19 8TS
vi

*In memory*
*of*
*Captain Roger Wykes-Sneyd*

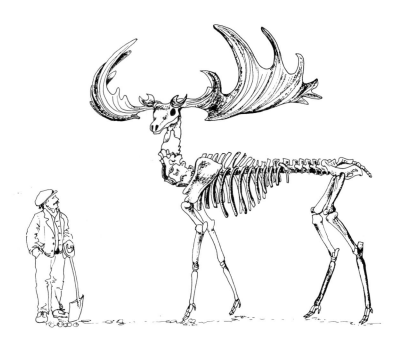

'*Wissett man meets prehistoric skeleton of giant deer.*' *It has been hypothesized that certain deer horns found in East Anglia, even in this area, may have originally belonged to the giant deer (megaloceros) that roamed Europe throughout the mesozoic ages, 180-70 million years ago. Skeletal remains were glacially transported here from deposits in the midlands half a million years ago.*

# Acknowledgments

We are indebted to the residents of Wissett, present or past, without whom this book could never have come about. We particularly thank everyone for their good humour in talking to us and for their generosity in lending us precious photographs and documents, and indeed other objects connected with the neighbourhood (Ewbank carpet-sweepers, Calvert's Carbolic Toothpowder, Roman pottery, even a prehistoric deer's horn).

Our especial gratitude must go to the late Captain Roger Wykes-Sneyd, to Dr Judith Middleton Stewart, Mr and Mrs Gerald Kiddy, Mr Adrian Talbot, Mr Mike Fordham and everyone at Halesworth & District Museum for their historical research. In addition, thanks are due to all the staff at the Beccles public library, to Chris and Peter Baron at Halesworth Bookshop, and to Pauline and Jim Hayward for their ingenuity in accessing strange and out-of-print books. We are deeply grateful to Margaret Colman and her shopful of rare books and curios in Beccles; to Bruce Pearce and friends who have procured valuable old directories and Waveney Valley farming magazines; to Adrian Goodman for allowing us to use extracts from the private journals of Lady Ottoline Morrell; to Ann Chown for many missing links in Wissett genealogies and chronologies; to Patricia Stanford, Karen Clement and Vicky Kemp for charming material about their forbears.

To all those connected with the technical side of book-production we owe particular thanks: to Julie Stoppard and Geoff Willis at New Thresholds, Beccles, for their computer skills; to The Adshop, Halesworth, for their photography and reprographic expertise; to our printers, the Pymar family and team at Technographic, Halesworth, for their patience and imaginative help before, during, and after printing.

# Contents

# Contents

# Illustrations

# Introduction

This book is an evocation of a village in the year 2000. It is a collection of local people's memories of their homes and families, their livelihoods and preoccupations, their hardships and exploits.

Many of the reminiscences are colourful, some are plain fanciful - but all are interwoven into Wissett folk-memory: nostalgic, funny, harsh.

The jigsaw of events in Wissett over the last two hundred years and more reflects the phenomenal hard work among those who ploughed, sowed, trampled the hemp, cut the withys, shod the horses, milked, tailored, cobbled, bartered and auctioned, thatched and milled, taught, learnt and prayed in what was essentially a mediaeval manorial system. Even the pews in the church were numbered in pecking order of their occupants. Some twenty-four farms and small-holdings eked out a living a hundred years ago; now there are barely half a dozen. The last Lordship of the Manor ended at the time of the Second World War.

This record of Wissett does not pretend to be what it isn't. It is neither history nor biography nor geography proper, but participates in all of these. Whilst we as editors have taken pains to reproduce faithfully everyone's stories, it is only fair to observe that one person's memory is markedly different from another's. Indeed, on different occasions, the same person may have entirely new perceptions of an event.

Even our documented sources (parish records, Kelly's and White's Directories, gravestones, early atlases, tithe lists and Suffolk histories) do not always concur. But that is the nature of information, whether oral or written. As George Ewart Evans (the remarkable Welshman who has chronicled so much of East Anglian life, and even included Wissett folk in his scripts) says, it raises the whole matter of what is history, and what is a recorder to note down? 'Often it is the trivial, the remark made on the side, the piece of gossip, that reveal the attitudes....that will be of the greatest value' in assessing more weighty facts. Evans goes on to observe, 'The anecdote, the tit-bit of gossip may well take him (ie the compiler or recorder) right into the heads of the people he is writing about.'

Inevitably there are large gaps in our narrative, as there are in people's memories. Over the last two years, we have pieced together as genuine a story of Wissett as our means allow, and can only apologize for omissions and unintentional errors.

We have followed a very simple structure in our 'Walk Through Wissett,' visiting each dwelling in turn. We start at the Halesworth end of the village, using the pre-1934 boundaries, and ending up at the Rumburgh end of Gray's Lane. We hope that, in spite of its shortcomings, this handbook captures the quite extraordinary character of Wissett in this millennium year.

Diana Fernando
Helen Flaxman

October 2000

# Wissett Place

Until 1934, this comfortable house with its two-acre pasture formed the easternmost boundary of Wissett at the corner of the Old Station Road and the Halesworth/Bungay Road. Geographically on the margin of the parish, Wissett Place was nonetheless very much part of the community, being the seat of the Pedgrift family of surgeons and benefactors through most of the nineteenth century.

By the 1830s, Dr William Henchman Pedgrift was the best-known surgeon of the district, and the most influential; he even had his own pew in Wissett Church - No 21. He and his wife Lucy had eleven verifiable children. The Wissett Burial Register has a doleful list of those who died young. One of William Henchman's daughters died at ten months, three sons died in their twenties or thirties, and four grandchildren in infancy. Of those who survived childhood, three remained at Wissett Place and started their own families there: Cornelius Shrofield (fifthborn in 1823) with his wife Charlotte; Ellen (sixthborn in 1824) with her husband John More; and Emma (seventhborn in 1826) who became Mrs Minell.

The 1881 census reveals that one of Cornelius Shrofield's daughters, Charlotte, had married a Stanford, and was staying at Wissett Place with her two sons, Eberfield Stanford, aged eleven and William, aged eight. Two more of the inmates of the day were Dr Cornelius Pedgrift's niece Rosetta Williams who was eight, and her father, James Williams, a commission agent. The household's maid was Anne Miller, a mere fourteen years old.

Cornelius Shrofield Pedgrift succeeded his father as surgeon at Wissett Place for almost fifty years. He was on the Wissett School Board for a number of sessions during the 1880s. By 1900, his widow is listed as the sole occupant and by 1908, new people had moved in: Henry Lawrence and entourage. John Lawn owned the house by 1916, but in all likelihood he let it out, while living off and on as a cattle-dealer at the other family seat: Broadway House. The next named occupant of Wissett Place is Frederick Woods, who was there briefly in the early 1920s. He was farm bailiff to John Lawn, and seems to be the same Mr Woods who moved to 25 The Street on retirement. A Miss Harvey is the last resident of Wissett Place to be mentioned before the reorganization of the Wissett boundaries in 1934. There are, however, various journalistic references to Wissett Place, including a wedding in 1960 at Wissett church between Frank Howlett and Josephine Lawn, niece of John Lawn of Wissett Place.

## Rock Cottage

This neat cottage, along the Old Station Road, remained within the Wissett parish until the East Suffolk Review Order of 1934. It is right by the level-crossing over the old Haddiscoe-Beccles-Halesworth railway line, which was established in 1851 and became part of the East Suffolk Railway in 1854. The original terminus was here with Rock Cottage on one side of the track and the old Station House on the other. Designed by Geoffrey Berkley, the line was used for a hundred years without an accident caused by engineering error. Different companies ran the trains over the century, but the line itself survived the Beeching Report in 1963 and is today used by Anglia Railways.

In the 1830s and 40s, the 'green fields all around,' that the present owners of Rock Cottage still remember, were then part of the estate of William Pattison, and the cottage was tenanted by Stephen Newson. Later Victorian occupants were Isaac Butcher with his wife Sarah, and William Thompson, listed in the 1881 census as 'gun maker,' who with his wife, Maris, lived alongside the Butchers in the other half of the cottage until the turn of the century. Then there was a Mrs Robertson, followed by the Fairweathers. Mrs Fairweather's father, Mr Peacock, owned much of the property on the outskirts of Halesworth, and probably bequeathed Rock Cottage to his daughter. Her husband ran the Bridge Street tobacconist's and newsagent's shop in Halesworth right through to the 1920s, and he was a favourite preacher at Wissett non-conformist chapel. By the 1960s, Mrs Fairweather's tenants at Rock Cottage were Mr and Mrs Ducker, who are still there today. Mrs Fairweather gave the cottage to them, and they live in the right side. Their daughter, Barbara King, lived in Beck Cottage in the 1990s. Mr and Mrs Anderson rented the left side until they moved a short while ago into Mill Road, Wissett.

## The Stud Bungalow, *(sometimes known as Manor Bungalow)*

This little bungalow built at the bottom of Wash Lane, on the west side, no longer exists, but played such a vivid part in the lives of Wissett people that it deserves a mention. It skirted the Spexhall/Wissett boundary and was associated with the Calverts of Spexhall Manor. Everyone who was here fifty years ago can remember the dashing Ralph Calvert, racing through Wissett in his open-top Lagonda, with Phyllis Calvert at his side, her hair flowing. She was never his wife, but she assumed his name for her professional career. She starred in the wartime Ealing and Gainsborough studio comedies, such as *Let George Do It*, with George Formby, and *The Man in Grey*, with Stewart Granger and James Mason.

The bungalow was built for the workers at Spexhall Manor. Nellie and Freddie Oxborough lived here awhile before moving into St Peter's Farmhouse, Wissett, and Cyril Maulden lodged here as a teenager with a Mrs Taylor. He shared the poky dank rooms with an evacuee boy called Colin Leach. In the 1950s, Reggie Elvin of Bleach Farm wanted to buy it for his tenant David Baker and his wife. That is what he did, although he had not foreseen that the Bakers would stay there for fifteen years.

In the 1990s, John Maynard, by then at Spexhall Manor, bought the place for £40,000, and promptly pulled it down.

This whole area round the bottom of Wash Lane is redolent with legend. Kevin Nunn, in his search to find which Wissett field was known as the 'King's Danger,' confirms that every local person he has spoken to says the same thing: that it was one of these fields near Mill Road and Wissett Road, by a bridge. Although opinions differ as to which of three possible bridges is meant, the one below Wash Lane is preferred, and, in a tradition rivalling the Hoxne claim, this is where King Edmund of East Anglia held his position against the Danes but was betrayed, captured and beheaded in 870. The neighbouring osier-beds are traditionally where Saxon kings were buried.

## Wissett Hall Cottage and The Cottage

These two cottages were built in about 1903 by the then owner of Wissett Hall, Mr Herbert Broom, (of Stanford, Broom & Stanford Real Estates in Halesworth) for his employees. Today Helen Hurren (née Agnes Hall) lives in The Cottage, which has been her home for most of her life, while her son Richard and his wife Julie live in Wissett Hall Cottage. Helen's parents, John and Agnes Hall, came to Wissett Hall Cottage with their two young daughters, Helen and Nora, in 1921 or thereabouts. John had been employed by Mr Walter Scrimgeour to oversee the gardens at Hemsby Hall in Norfolk. When the Scrimgeours had moved from Hemsby to take up residence at Wissett Hall, John and family had come with them - John to be head gardener at Wissett Hall, with seven gardeners working under him. Before the move, John would cycle down to Wissett Hall at weekends to tend the garden while the house was made ready.

*William Nunn with 'Wissett Frederic,' his first prize Red Poll, 24.4.1936.*

Helen Hall married a Wissett man, William Hurren, in 1937 after meeting him at a dance in Rumburgh village hall (known as 'the hut'). William was born at Hill House Farm in Wissett, but the family moved to Halesworth in 1912 to set up Hurren's Butchers, a shop that is still there and is now run by Helen's son Dick. After their marriage, Helen and William moved to Halesworth where Helen remained while William was away during the war. Afterwards, William's parents retired to Norfolk, leaving the butchers business in the hands of Helen and William, who moved into the flat above the shop. Meanwhile, The Cottage at Wissett was occupied by James (Jimmy) and Helen Nunn. Jimmy was employed by the Scrimgeours as horseman at Wissett Hall and Helen did dressmaking. Their daughter Joyce (now Mrs Charlie Mouser) remembers moving here, from Rose Cottage, when she was about six years old, probably in 1926. She recalls how good the Scrimgeours were to all their employees. They would have the cottages redecorated regularly and would leave wallpaper samples for her parents to choose which ones they wanted. Mrs Scrimgeour would bring around, every Christmas, a cracker for all the children.

Joyce remembers what was one of the happiest days of her childhood: the celebrations for King George V's Silver Jubilee in 1935. There were 'fun and frolics' on the meadow in front of Whitehouse Farm. Incredible amounts of food were consumed, with sports afterwards. Another vivid memory is of The Duke of York coming to Halesworth and changing trains for Southwold. He came with a group of underprivileged children from London every year and camped on Southwold Common up until he became King in 1936.

Joyce's parents, Jimmy and Helen Nunn, moved to Halleluia Cottage in 1957. John and Agnes Hall, still living in Wissett Hall Cottage, bought The Cottage for £500, so that their daughter Helen and son-in-law William Hurren could live next door to them. In later years, long after settling comfortably into The Cottage, Helen and William had the opportunity, in turn, to buy Wissett Hall Cottage, where their son Dick and his wife Julie now live. Sadly William Hurren died in December 1999, just after his Diamond Wedding Anniversary and his ninetieth birthday.

## Wissett Hall

Wissett Hall is a fine timber-framed brick house set in twenty-two acres of land. There has probably been a house on this site since at least the sixteenth century. The present house is described by the Department of the Environment's Schedule of Listed Buildings as: 'Early seventeenth century core, with late Victorian enlargements by Herbert Broom. Timber-framed, encased in red-brick, mainly nineteenth century, but with some sections of Tudor brick; the central range is jettied and tile-hung on the upper floor; hipped plaintiled roofs. Two storeys; complex plan...Linked to the north side of the house is a small two-storey early twentieth-century circular tower by Louis Sarel... early twentieth-century timbered and panelled interior: two bays of the original seventeenth-century house, with plain exposed ceiling-joists are visible. The ground floor windows on the porch and the dentil details probably also by Sarel.'

The man responsible for building Wissett Hall or rebuilding it in the early seventeenth century was probably Ciprian Sallowes. Ciprian died and was buried in Wissett in March 1630. In his will, he left to his wife Elizabeth (née Browne) 'all that my messuage or tenement wherein I now dwell....as it is lying and being in Wissett between the lands of Henrie Morton Esquier called Blenches on the part of the east, and the kings highwaie leading from Hallisworth to Spexhall toward to the west.' The placing of the property on the 'kings highway' between Halesworth and Spexhall to the west confirms that Ciprian Sallowes lived at Wissett Hall; it would then have been known simply as the house of Ciprian Sallowes.

After Elizabeth died in October 1653, Wissett Hall went to their daughter Sara. This heiress had by then married Henry Stebbings of Earl Soham and had four children: Henry, Elizabeth, Cyprian and Sara. Sara Stebbings died only a few years after her mother, Elizabeth, in July 1660, aged forty-one. Her son Henry took possession of Wissett Hall (it was referred to as Winlards, and in the 1840 Tithe entry, the field in which Wissett Hall is sited was still called Winlards) in 1663. Henry too died young, in 1668, and left the Hall to his two sisters, Elizabeth (now married to Richard Jenkinson) and Sara.

At the time of the Hearth Tax return of 1674, Henry Stebbings senior was occupying the largest house in Wissett, with ten hearths. If this was Wissett Hall it was already an impressive building. In 1726 Elizabeth Jenkinson died and her son Richard Jenkinson

*Mr and Mrs Walter Scrimgeour of Wissett Hall, 1930s*

was the heir, and on his death in 1749, his son and namesake inherited the hall. This Richard Jenkinson and his wife Eleanor lived in London and they decided to sell his rural property in Wissett on 12 October 1751. The buyer was Thomas Spalding, a yeoman of Wissett. Thomas kept the property until February 1769, when it was transferred to his son Thomas Spalding junior. This young man and his wife Rachel disposed of the property a few months later to Benjamin Murrel (or Murrill, as he appears later) a tanner of Beccles. A stark note in Wissett Burial Register for 1813 states that a Thomas Spalding, 45, was 'found drowned in a pond in parish of Wissett. Lunacy.' Whether this was an unfortunate son of Rachel and Thomas is not known. Meanwhile, Benjamin Murrel died in 1782 and his property passed to his daughter Elizabeth Murrill (later Chamber). Elizabeth sold her land in Wissett to John Woodcock the younger of Halesworth, in 1799. John died in 1800 or 01 and his wife Elizabeth became the owner, although she appears never to have lived here as she was living in Ipswich. On 23 November 1835 she sold Winlards to Isaac Wilcox for the sum of £320.

By April 1841 Isaac had died and in the 1841 Tithe record the estate is listed as a farm of 108 acres in the hands of the executors of Isaac Wilcox but occupied by Jonathan Howlett (an auctioneer). In the 1844 White's Directory it is referred to as Hill House but still occupied by Mr Howlett. By 1867 he is the owner and it is thought that he then changed the name to Wissett Hall. He never married, but his household included his mother, Mary Howlett, until she died in 1861; a nurse, Harriet Mayhew; a servant, Frederick Barber; and the housekeeper Cordelia Mannall. Jonathan died on 29 May 1887 at the age of eighty-six and was buried in Wissett churchyard. In 1888 the whole farm plus a further 662 acres, which Mr Howlett owned in Wissett and several other parishes, were put up for sale by his executors.

In 1892 the estate was owned by Mr Aaron Leathers ( a farmer and corn merchant from Diss) and his wife Mary Ann. By the turn of the century it was owned by Herbert Broom. It was at this time that major additions to the house were built, possibly including the tower. Herbert Broom owned Wissett Hall until 1912 when it became the property of Henry Otto Nicholson Shaw. In 1919 it was put up for auction but was bought by Private Treaty by John Barclay Rose. Mr Rose conveyed it to W Scrimgeour Esq on 21 March 1921 for £11,000. Walter Scrimgeour had been a member of the stock exchange since 1878. He and his wife Elizabeth, who were both elderly, came from Hemsby Hall with their daughter Marjorie. They had moved as they were not happy about the building of a holiday village near Hemsby. They had a pedigree Red Poll cattle herd which won them numerous awards; they even exported some of their cattle to America. They employed plenty of local people. Domestic servants included a cook, kitchenmaid and scullerymaid, head parlourmaid and under parlourmaid, housemaid and under housemaid, a lady's maid for both women and possibly a manservant and butler. Outside there were eight gardeners, two chauffeurs, a head steward, a horseman and cowman. They are the ones remembered! Marjorie, who never married, was a stalwart in the Brownies, Guides and Rangers. What used to be a brick cheese house behind The Hall was turned into a hut for the meetings. It is still there but no longer used for that purpose.

Mr Scrimgeour died in May 1937 aged eighty-five. His trustees were his three sons, Hugh Carron, Stuart and Humphrey, none of whom took up residence. In 1955 the larger part of the land was sold off to BE Norman for the sum of £5250. Stuart Scrimgeour died on 10 May 1956 and in August, Wissett Hall was sold to James Walter Smith. James

Smith sold the property on 3 October 1961 to Michael Taylor Young from Leeds. Ten years later, The Hall changed hands again and was sold to Mr and Mrs Noe Glasman of Beccles. The price was £28,000.

Caven Investment Incorporation, of Panama City, bought The Hall on 13 June 1976 and they sold it on 21 March 1980 to Stanley Alexander Williams. Alex Williams had been an architect in the Middle East and owned a garage and public house near Bungay. Associated with the Williams Formula I racing cars, Alex was also a collector of prestige and old cars. He made improvements to the house and added the swimming pool. Mr John Maynard (of M&H Plastics, Beccles) was the next to buy The Hall, in May 1983, and he did extensive works on the grounds, creating the lake and helicopter pad and planting numerous trees. Mr Maynard sold in 1990 and moved to Spexhall Manor. The present owner is Mr Colin Robert Holmes (connected with the company of Dencora in Beccles) who lives part of the time in Beccles.

## Birches

This bungalow was built between 1968 and 1972 to house the pigman and his family who worked in the piggeries at Wissett Hall. When it was first built it consisted of a hall, three bedrooms, a bathroom, small kitchen and a living room. In 1972 it, along with pig buildings and fattening pens, was sold to Eastside Farms Ltd., and was then called East Side.

The occupants changed and a flat-roofed extension was added, making it a six-bedroomed bungalow. The kitchen was extended, a laundry room added, and the smallish living room was converted into a largish living/dining room. The bungalow was bought in 1986 by John and Jill Maynard of Wissett Hall, and they sold it on to Frank and Elizabeth Offord in 1987. Frank and Elizabeth changed the name to 'Croydon' after the village in Cambridgeshire where they had met.

The present owners, David and Jenny Ball, have lived here since 1995. They have changed the name yet again to Birches (having planted four birch trees in the garden) and they have also made alterations. Two of the bedrooms have been made into a larger bedroom, and one bedroom and a storeroom have been made into an office and studio.

Jenny and David have done a lot of work in the garden. There is now a herb garden, wild-life pond, gravel garden, rose garden, trellises, shade gardens, terracing and shrub garden. When others were converting outside lavatories into storerooms or knocking them down, they had one built at the back of the house.

David is a retired local government officer and Jenny is a retired librarian. David is the parish clerk for Wissett and tests courses for the Open University Business School. He studies Ancient Greek in his spare time! Jenny is editor of *The Wissett Web*, the village newsletter. She is also secretary of the Parochial Church Council and the Wissett/Spexhall WI and helps to run the Wissett Bloomers, the garden club. In her spare time, she paints on silk to sell at craft fairs, and is a keen photographer. The Balls have both been active on the Millennium Committee and get involved in any fund-raising event for the village.

## Oaklands *(formerly Hall Farm)*

It is believed this house was built by Herbert Broom in 1908 or so. When Walter Scrimgeour was in Wissett Hall he employed two chauffeurs: Mr Hilling as head chauffeur and Mr Freddie Read as under chauffeur  Mr Hilling lived here at the time and would drive Mr and Mrs Scrimgeour around in the Rolls Royce. Mrs Mouser (née Nunn) remembers both chauffeurs looking very smart in their dark grey livery. After Mr Hilling left, Charlie Fleming became chauffeur-cum-handyman and lived here with his wife Lily (née Block). They had two sons and a daughter, Beryl, who remembers moving when she was about five to No 7 Brickhill Cottage.

Mr Bertie and Mrs May Norman bought this house, along with Hall Farm Lodge and eighty acres, in 1955 when Wissett Hall was sold. They came from Denham, near Eye, with their son Bertie and his wife Doreen. Bertie and Doreen moved into Hall Farm Lodge. Bertie senior died in 1962 and in 1968 his widow, May, moved into Hall Farm Lodge, while Bertie junior moved into Hall Farm with his wife Doreen and their two sons. In 1992 they decided to semi-retire and so had a bungalow built next door. They moved, taking the name Hall Farm with them.

Mary and Peter Copperthwaite bought the house next, naming it Oaklands. They moved in on 14 November 1992 with their daughter Rachel and son Joseph, coming from Billericay in Essex. They have done extensive work on the house and garden since arriving. Peter is a wizard with a welding rod and works for Hammonds Repair Shop in Halesworth. Mary does office work in Bramfield and Thetford. Both are very involved in village life, Mary being a parish councillor and engaged in the production of *The Wissett Web*.

## Hall Farm

This is a relatively new bungalow, built by  Bertie and Doreen Norman  for their semi-retirement in 1992. They still live here with their son Kevin, who works the farm with his brother Peter, helped by Bertie.

## Hall Farm Lodge

This house was built in about 1923 by Walter Scrimgeour, and a Mr Matthews appears to have lived here from the start. He was the head steward at Wissett Hall. By 1945, Alice Nunn had arrived here with her family. Her husband Willie was cowman at The Hall under Mr Matthews, looking after the pedigree Red Poll herd. Willie's brother, Johnny, reminds us that there was no insurance protection in those days, so when Willie was seriously injured by one of the Red Polls and had to have his leg off, he had no compensation except death.

The fourteen 'boxes' where the cattle were housed and milked still stand behind The

Lodge. At some stage they are thought to have been used as racing stables by a Captain Percy A Whitaker. With his stud groom, Arthur Wright, he would put the horses on the train at Halesworth and take them to Newmarket.

When Wissett Hall was sold in 1955, this is the house that the Normans bought. The very next day after the younger generation of Normans had moved in here, their son Peter was born. In 1968 Bertie junior and his wife Doreen swapped houses with their mother/mother-in-law May, as she was now widowed. In 1988, after May had died, Bertie and Doreen's son and daughter-in-law, Peter and Anne, plus their children Ian and Lisa, moved from Spexhall into The Lodge, adding an extension at the same time. They now work the farm along with Peter's brother Kevin and helped by Bertie. They have a pig fattening unit and haulage business, as well as farming several acres for Mr Maynard at Spexhall Manor.

## Grove Farm: *Domus, Willow Barn, Barn House and Grove Farm House*

The early history of the individual dwellings listed above was the history of Grove Farm, which until the 1950s was under one ownership.

The old farmhouse itself, now Grove Farm House, has a timber-framed front section built circa 1750 and a brick-built back section added in about 1850. In the 1830s, the estate was tied up with big Fleetwood and Parkyns manorial lands in Cheditson. The half-French George Parkyns (whose descendants still hold the lordship of Cheditson) owned Grove Farm, which comprised some 112 acres of largely arable fields. It was farmed by Robert Tacon of Wissett (who married Ann Whiting in Thorington church on 19 July 1832).

According to the 1881 census, Francis Chambers was by then the head farmer, aided by his wife Mary, his young niece Mary Howard, and the fourteen-year-old servant Caroline Mouser. By 1892, Grove Farm was run by John Ingate, whose family had branches at Linstead, Cheditson and Walpole. From roughly 1900 up to the First World War, John Edward Ingate was in charge of the farm. Descendants of the Ingates still farm in the Cheditson area. Mary Ingate, in between her busy life as a farmer's wife, won an award with Macmillan publishers in the 1970s for the first of her unusual crime novels, *The Sound of the Weir*. Meanwhile, back in the late 1800s the Hurren family, who had another farm in Wissett, were also farming at Grove Farm. Canna ('Caney' - even 'Cain not Abel') Hurren (son of George who had farmed as well as run The Swan public house in the late 1800s) was managing Grove Farm during the 1920s. His successors in the 1930s were William Cana Hurren and William Hurren. The farm is remembered for its dairy; people from Halesworth would walk there to get their milk.

At the end of the Second World War, the new people at Grove Farm were Mabel and Leonard Everett, and during the 1950s, Major and Mrs Galloway with their two children took the farm over.

The next owner was Mr Mike Taylor Young, who also owned Wissett Hall. As his 'third pig-man' he hired David Addison-Carter, a Norfolk man. This was in the late 1960s. So David, his wife Clodagh, and their three young children: Davina, Louise and Ross, moved from Wymondham to Grove Farm. As Mr Addison-Carter was now the foreman, he and his family lived in the old farmhouse. The two men started a pig breeding unit of Elite Hybrid pigs for Captain Chute of Bulhams.

The Addison-Carters had only been at the farm for a couple of years when Mike Taylor Young suddenly announced that he was leaving. He put the cheque books and accounts down on the table in front of David and said, with words to this effect: 'You'd better run this farm. I've bought a farm in Bridgwater, Somerset, and I'm moving there now.' Which, according to Ross, is what he did.

The Addison-Carters did a heroic job in turning the farm round. In 1974, they bought in several acres of pig-units, and ran the main farm site of sixty acres for the next twenty years. The remaining fifty acres were sold away firstly to David Baker and then to Bertie Norman. The children grew up and Louise left to become a civil engineer. Disaster struck in the mid-1990s when both parents died, in spite of Davina's constant care.

The old pig-styes to the east of the big barn were made into two homes: Domus and Willow Barn. Having moved into Domus in order to convert the barn into a spectacular homestead, Davina and her husband David Pointon eventually were able to move in to their transformed barn, now Barn House. Domus was sold to Shirley Myland and her husband Bernard, a retired flight planner with Qantas Airlines. Willow Barn became the home of Ross (a haulage contractor) and his partner, Rachel (an assistant at Durrant's Estate Agents).

Davina and David have sold Barn House to Mary Montague from Blythburgh, while the owners of the original farmhouse, Grove Farm House, are Susan and Peter Duckett, who came from Halesworth in 1997 with their children: Alex (now 14), Rory (8) and Georgia (6). Sue lectures at Lowestoft in Childcare and Education, while Peter runs his second-hand record and tape shop. In whatever spare time they have, Sue and Peter are busy replacing windows, doors and floors. They have made a wildlife pond in the garden which has become a habitat for great crested newts.

A ghost in the form of a White Lady has been seen by the Addison-Carters. One night the lady left the house through a newly replaced bedroom window that had previously been nailed shut.

*Mill House windmill reconstructed.*

# Camelot

According to the 1839-40 Tithe map, Robert Baas of Chediston Hall owned this cottage, and a certain George Foyster lived here with 'another.' In Halesworth parish church, the stained glass window in the north aisle is dedicated to Baas, who died in 1875 in his ninety-eighth year. A glance at the 1881 census shows that the March family lived in the cottage then, Elliss March having the title: 'Engine Driver Threshing Machine Attendant.' Another couple appear to be living here at the same time: Frederick Mayhew, labourer, and his wife Mary, plus a 'boarder,' Frederick Pinfold. All three are listed as having been born at Bulcamp, which was the workhouse for the district.

The site was associated with the neighbouring Grove Farm, and known as Grove Farm Cottage. In the early twentieth century, Beryl McMorran's grandparents, Mr and Mrs ('Nana') Block, moved here from Chediston Street with their growing family. They had many a ghostly tale to tell, particularly about the shaggy dog, alias The Black Shuck, who would mysteriously appear on Mill Road and run alongside their bicycles between the mill and Wissett Lodge. Harmless enough, but eerie. When Ivy, the youngest child, was about eleven months old, the Blocks moved to Mill House. William and Phyllis Hammond came to live in one side of the cottage, while Tom and Percy Sallis (or Sallows) lived in the other side. Percy was an old army cook and Tom his father. Dick Colby remembers them as a couple of real characters.

The cottage name was changed to 'Camelot' in the 1950s by the Greenaways, who still live there

# Mill Cottage

This was a freehold cottage and garden dating back to at least 1800. The present owner, Mrs Daphne Ritchie, found a George III halfpenny preserved in the original dining-room wall. In common with many of the farm cottages of that era, this one was divided into two dwellings. It was owned in the 1840s by Elisha Cullingford; and by 1881 housed William Morris, an 'agricultural labourer,' and his wife Honor in one side; and in the other, the retired farmers Joseph and Susan Bishop. The cottage changed owners several times during the following century.

By the 1940s, William ('Uncle Winter') Oxborough, son of Nellie and Freddie, lived there with his wife, Mary, and children. His son George William, who had been a fisherman, was in the navy in the Second World War when his ship went down. There is a plaque to him in Wissett church. William's daughter Vera married Sid Aldridge at The Swan Inn.

Mary could not bear William's pipe. She made her husband sit in the cupboard beside the fire to smoke his 'County Shag' made by Churchman's of Ipswich. From a very early age, Mary had had snow-white hair and walked with a stick. She would hail her youthful sister-in-law Annie Oxborough across the crowded Halesworth street with: 'O Good God, gal Annie! How old you begin to look!' or, 'O gal Annie, it must be lovely to die!'

Later, the cottage was bought by John Leach, whose mother was a property developer. William Bird was living there at the time, and was reluctant to move out when the place

11

*Mrs Daphne Ritchie and Mr Ernie Block, Mill House 1983.*

was taken over for holiday renting. When builders came to renovate it and knock a wall down, the tale goes, William was in there having breakfast. His wife had died miserably of cancer, as had one daughter. In the end, William moved across the road and claimed squatters' rights in the pit at the corner of the Aldous's field opposite Mill Cottage. He had two caravans at the least, six Robin Reliant cars and a motor-bus. Daphne Ritchie and her daughter, Hope, still remember once helping him push a sideboard through the end window of the caravan that he lived in. He was, apparently, very attracted to bargains, even ones that proved not very useful to himself, such as the huge pile of pillows he was spotted struggling with on one occasion.

Daphne has been a staunch member of the village community. She has many a tale to tell about flood and storm, fund-raising efforts, Treacle Fairs, local and eccentric elders of the village, church functions and hospital visitings to the sick and needy. In her sitting-room is a wonderful doll's house, about five feet high, made for her by her husband Bill. The doll's furniture is exquisite, as are the display cabinets of miniature treasures round Daphne's walls. One of the most remarkable escapades in Bill's life at Mill Cottage was his trip to India in 1979, departing from snowbound Wissett on a toboggan. Every possible exit from the village was blocked, but nonetheless Bill managed to reach his plane with time to spare. He rang up Daphne from Heathrow to say 'I'm here!' before flying off to his Jat Regiment (Indian Army) Veterans' Reunion. Bill - Major William David Ritchie MC - died in 1993, but his memory endures.

# Mill House

There were at least three windmills in Wissett in the Middle Ages. According to the 'Inquisition' (inquest or audit) after the death of William de Nerford in 1301, two windmills were 'let out to rent' at £1 6s 8d per annum.

The footings of the mill on this site can still be made out at the end of the garden. The mill was built in 1835, as is evident from a notice of sale in the *Suffolk Chronicle* of 28 November 1835:

*To be sold by private contract. A new-built WINDMILL, just ready for work, and a comfortable dwelling house, situate at Wissett.....The mill contains 4 floors, 2 pairs of stones, patent sails, and flour machine. If the said mill be not sold quickly, it will be let....Apply to J. Harrison, at the mill.*

There were several types of mill, the earliest being the post mill, with its great oak post on which the body or 'buck' containing the milling machine turned to face the wind. Its canvas-covered sails were manoeuvred by the miller leaning on the tailpole that jutted out through the steps at the rear. When the fantail was invented in 1745, the sails turned into the wind automatically.

The tower mill with its brick tower tarred to keep out the wet became popular in East Anglia. A variation was the smock mill, with its wooden tower painted white: a fanciful likeness of the old countryman's attire.

The mill here at Mill House was a tower mill. According to the 1839-41 Tithe records, it was owned by Samuel Farrow and run first by John Cable or Keable, then William Scarff Kett by 1847. The *Suffolk Chronicle* of 1 October 1853 contains a notice offering the mill and house to be sold, or let, via Kett, who later worked Wenhaston watermill and post mill. In 1855, Samuel Bryant is listed as 'farmer' and 'miller,' to be succeeded by the Bishop family at the millhouse. William Bishop is a 'cornmiller' by 1873, and by 1875 he is 'miller and overseer.' According to the 1881 census, William's family included Mary Ann his wife, three sons: William, Ernest and Harry, and two daughters: Carry who was four, and Rosa, just three. Their servant, Julia Chout, was fifteen and came from Rickwell, Essex. William Bishop had already been joined by an assistant miller, Samuel Jordan, who had originally come from Knodishall, but who, before moving into the millhouse, lived next door. Samuel and his family were ensconced in the millhouse by 1892, renting from the same Farrow family that had bought the mill in the 1830s.

Recently, Karen Clement, great-granddaughter of Samuel Jordan, provided Wissett with a fascinating link to Sarah Jordan, Samuel and Mary Ann Jordan's youngest child of the four who survived infancy. Sarah, born in 1886, attended Wissett school (where now the village hall stands) and Karen still possesses one of Sarah's immaculately hand-written exercise books from the school year 1898-9. Sarah grew up to marry Samuel Carter, a baker in Southwold. The young couple emigrated to Canada, and their children settled in British Columbia, where Karen still lives. She remembers her grandmother Sarah as an exceptionally kind lady, with many fond tales of life as a child in 'silly Suffolk.'

At last the estate was auctioned in 1904; on the 7 July, as 'Lot 2' the mill was described as the 'capital brick and boarded Tower Windmill,' and was bought by William Allen, who had been the tenant.

The mill remained powered by wind until 1912 at least, but by 1916 it had been converted to steam power. The last date that the miller, still Allen, is mentioned is 1922.

Thereafter, the millhouse no longer had a working mill, for shortly afterwards the Block family arrived here to live. Ivy Cullingford (née Block) remembers the mill had no sails. Her parents had eight children: Ernie, Jim, Eric, Lily, Bob, Leonard, Wilfred and herself, the youngest. The eldest son, Ernie, who passed away in his eighties a few years ago, is remembered with fondness, particularly by Daphne Ritchie next door at Mill Cottage. Many and varied were Ernie's comments on life and folk-wisdom!

His brother Jim died on his forty-second birthday; and Leonard had gone into the Navy, which had been a hard life: many sailors who did not die in the war died of TB. Ivy, now a lively seventy-year-old, lives in Bramfield.

The present owners, Letitia (Rosemary) and John Riches, bought Mill House after Ernie's death.

*Samuel Jordan, miller, in the 1880s*

## Heronsgill

Mrs Pippa Dorling, who has not long left her home here, named it after the herons that still haunt the streams that flow down to the Beck in the dips below the road. This property is listed in the 1839-40 Tithe return as 'tenement and yards' with a 'drift' (now part of Millcroft) owned by John Crabtree and occupied by Henry Muddett 'and another.'

In the course of its history, it was home to many farmworkers, sometimes several families at a time. It appears that not only the Jordans lived here before moving to the millhouse, but that they shared the premises with two other couples: Cornelius and Elizabeth Hunt, and John and Mary Plutcher. Cornelius Hunt was a master-thatcher and grandfather to the characterful 'Nellus' Hunt of No 2 The Street.

Occasionally, the two dwellings became one dwelling plus a byre. Pippa reminisces that a cow lived in the west end of her cottage, according to the childhood memories of Phyllis Green and her brother Phillip Ball. Phillip used to be taken for walks by his father across the fields from Rectory Street, Halesworth. They would see the cow peering out at them from what is now the dining room.

Local ladies now in their seventies talk of a Mr Hood who inhabited one of the Millcroft cottages for a little while. His two daughters were nicknamed The Heavenly Twins because they used to walk back and forth along Halesworth Thoroughfare of a Saturday night, parading themselves, while ostensibly looking in the shops - which in those heady days stayed open until 8.30pm.

After the war, Mrs ('Nana') Block, mother to Ernie and grandmother to Beryl McMorran, bought the cottage for £50. She died in 1959, aged seventy-five.

The Lamberts, Miles and Armorel, who lived at Ash Tree farm, bought the cottage and considerably modernized it. When Pippa took it over in the early 1990s, she added her studio in the garden and, as an inventive artist, transformed the interior with prints, paintings, pottery and flowers.

The newest owners, the Andersons, have just arrived from Rock Cottage. They ran the Quaker School in Saffron Walden, Mr Anderson being the headmaster.

## Millcroft

This lovely thatched cottage dates from around 1700. The earliest deeds are stamped 1732, when the property was owned by Robert and Elizabeth Clarke. The next known owner, taken from the 1841 Tithe records, is John Crabtree, with William Hunt in occupation.

At one time the place was divided into two and possibly could have been farmworkers' cottages for Whitehouse Farm. The 1881 census notes a James Jackson, 'agricultural labourer,' and his wife, Sara, as living somewhere between Heronsgill and Whitehouse Farm, without naming the actual dwelling. An additional mystery surrounds the exact position of the little 'sideways on' cottage that stood in the 'drift' or present driveway to the right of the Millcroft garages fronting the road, by the artesian well (which was a wind-driven water-pump). In the 1920s the Couch family lived there, and kept goats. The two children, Eunice and Raymond Couch, went to Wissett school.

In 1945 Millcroft was occupied by Charles and Gertrude Blinkhorn. Charlie Blinkhorn was a dealer renowned for the sheer variety of stock he would buy up - which at one point included the neighbouring cottage (Heronsgill). He needed a device for getting the tenants to vacate the cottage. He it was who installed the cow with her calf in the western half of the cottage. 'That'll get the buggars out!' he is supposed to have muttered.

A widower named Colonel Scott, allegedly something of a philanderer, owned the house for some time before it was bought by Dick and Mary Colby in 1947. Dick worked for Stanford Broom & Stanford. The couple lived here for fourteen years, during which time they had the roof rethatched by a Mr Rackham. Dick and Mary sold to a Mr White in 1961 and moved to Chediston. Mr White sold on to Mr and Mrs Warburton who lived here for ten years and did much restoration work. In 1980 Ernie and Evelyn Woolnough arrived. They remained in the house for eight and a half years, before moving into the bungalow that they built for themselves in their grounds. In 1989, having rented out Millcroft for a time, they sold it to Jeremy Fletcher-Morris, who is still the present owner.

## Sandy Hills

This is the bungalow that Ernie and Evelyn Woolnough were busy building in 1987 in the grounds of Millcroft, then their home. Ernie is one of the most enterprising of people, and has arranged entertainments at many a harvest supper and played music at many a carol-singing evening. He and Evelyn, who have three children: Lyn, Paul and James, and four grandchildren, have been wholly committed to the village. Ernie, active in starting the Community Council in 1989, was on the parish council for several years and in 1991 was instrumental in obtaining a grant to buy a bowling mat and bowls - this was the beginning of the Wissett Bowls Club. Along with John Howlett, Adrian Talbot and Matthew Wetmore, Ernie organized the first Treacle Fair in 1989 and continued to be involved with each fair thereafter until the last one in 1995. Some five years ago he applied for and got another grant for the extension on the village hall. Evelyn does a great deal of work for the church and is often seen helping some of the elderly members of the village, taking them shopping or whatever is needed. Meanwhile, Ernie can be spotted these days either up in his hot air balloon or his 'powerchute.'

## Bonners Farm

It is thought that this house, or parts of it, are around three hundred years old. There are some interior walls made of lath and plaster. Possibly it had been at one stage two semi-detached cottages. The 1841 Tithe map indicates that Mr Edmund William Hartopp owned the farm with 434 acres, and that it was managed by Mr John Tillott. The 1881 census lists a Hurrens Farm, but not a Bonners, although the positioning looks about right for both farms to be one and the same. A family of agricultural labourers are named: John Hauser, his wife Emma and six children: David, Ellen, Alfred, Albert, Frederick and Emma, ranging in descending order from sixteen to one year old.

Mr Samuel Button junior was here at Bonners from the early 1900s until about 1925, when Mr Charles Crake is noted in Kelly's Directory as being the owner. By 1929 the Kent brothers, Bob and Jo, were farming here, while Bob and his wife also ran the village shop in Wissett Street. During the war, a Lancaster bomber crashed into nearby 'Hurren's Field' with a full load of bombs. The explosion caused massive damage to this house and many others. By 1945, John and Maria De'ath were at Bonners with their two sons.

Geoff and Christine Hall lived here from 1959 to 1969, succeeded by Mr and Mrs Roy Nicholls until 1982. The Nicholls family then moved to France and sold to Mr Aldous of Chediston Hall. By now the farm was reduced to 160 acres and farmed by the Tannington Group for Mr Aldous, whose son Peter is living in the house now. He is a surveyor and also a Waveney District Conservative councillor.

# Whitehouse Farm

This old farmhouse dates from the 1500s with additions made in the 1600s and 1700s. From roughly 1650-1750 a family named Hervey lived here, that progressed from yeoman farmer to gentleman farmer then back to yeoman farmer in three generations. From the early 1800s to 1850 Robert Aldred, who had a linen factory in Halesworth, lived here and owned 125 acres. In the 1841 Tithe record he is listed as owning and occupying Whitehouse Farm together with what was later called 'Halleluia Cottage,' while managing Bond's and Bleach Farms with James Aldred, probably his brother.

He was a member of the committee formed for the rebuilding of the Independent meeting house in Halesworth in 1834 and was chosen as deacon in 1837. His mother Mrs Mary Aldred had been a member there in 1797. Before an organ was obtained for the meeting house, the singing was led by Mr Aldred with the aid of a tuning fork. He became one of the trustees of the newly built Wissett chapel and was 'a great worker for the cause there. At the opening of the Wissett chapel in 1841, Robert provided 'a spread in a tent near his house.' He moved to Stoven at the end of the 1840s, afterwards to Norwich. He died in 1865.

The 1881 census indicates that Thomas Lincoln lived here with his wife Mary, their two daughters Beatrice and Edith, and their servant Betsy Bird. As well as the main farm, two sets of cottages that housed farm labourers are labelled 'Whitehouse Farm Cottages,' which conceivably refer to Halleluia Cottage. The tenants of one are listed as: John Flatt and his wife Sabriear, plus five children no older than fifteen years - Eliza, Caroline, Maria, William and Elizabeth. The second set of cottages accommodated the Page parents, Samuel and Ellen, plus their small daughters - Ellen, Beya (sic) and Emma; it also provided a sanctuary for a young fisherman's wife, Rosetta Wollage, and her baby son Alonzo Charles.

By 1894 the farm was owned by Mr William and Mrs Florence Whatling. The bridge over the Beck at the Wissett end of Mill Road was called Whatling's Arch after William and Florence, who moved away in 1919 to The Elms in Halesworth. Their son John, his wife 'Prunie' and their son William (who was two at the time) took over the farm. John was a keen cricketer and when he left in 1926 the

*Beatrice ('Prunie') Whatling at Whitehouse Farm before World War One*

17

*Heinz, a prisoner-of-war from Dresden, in 1946, holding the baby Joan Meek.*

Wissett Cricket Team presented him with a handsome wall clock. Although John moved to Laxfield, he kept the farm machinery, and continued to do much of the steam thrashing for many of the Wissett farms. By 1926, Edward Guy Godbold had taken Whitehouse Farm on.

Peter Cutts remembers a huge flood at harvest-time in the stackyard (now Rickyards), when Mr Godbold's corn - already cut, bound and 'shock up' - was swept entirely away. Swine fever was a problem before the war no less than now. Godbold's men, as was the general practice, shot all the pigs and dug them into a big pit on the farmland and shovelled quicklime over the top.

Cyril Maulden recounts a strange experience he had as a lad in one of Godbold's fields. It was Saturday, 4 October 1930, about 7pm, when Cyril was blackberrying in the field known as Church Hill, approached through the gate opposite Rose Cottage. Cyril remembers it was October because of the 'shrivelled up blackberries.' He looked up to see a huge airship. 'It was gliding along lovely,' recalls Cyril. 'The R101. It was written on the side.' The next day, those with wireless sets heard the shattering news of the R101's crash near Beauvais in France, on her maiden flight to India.

The farm changed hands, probably just before the war. The Slater family took it on, with their two other farms: Wissett Lodge, and Whitehouse Farm, Rumburgh. Mrs Annie Patience Slater offered her daughter, Margaret Meek, one of the three farms, and Margaret chose Whitehouse, Wissett. Annie came to live with Margaret and her husband, Stuart, who was in the local Home Guard during the war. Two daughters were born: Joan, then Ann; and apart from the family, the lively household included Daphne the housekeeper and her young daughter Virginia, a nurse for Mrs Annie Slater, and a prisoner of war from Dresden called Heinz, who made the Meek girls ingenious wooden toys. The farm hands included John Hall, Colin Doughty, Dick Foster and Jimmy Laws.

The Meeks were great fund-raisers and used to hold sporting events in the field behind the stackyard. Mrs Meek was fascinated by local history and archaeology, and helped local groups. Joan decided to launch her career in pop music. She sang with Tom Paxton and Peter Noone before making her own recordings. Ann lives in London, while Joan has pursued her musical aptitude, and teaches piano in Norfolk.

In the April of 1969 Roger and Katharine Wykes-Sneyd came from Hampshire with their four children: Ralph (who was in the navy, later to command the *Invincible*'s helicopter squadron 820 during the Falklands War), Hector (a chartered surveyor), and two daughters, Cordelia and Honora. Captain Wykes-Sneyd was in the Royal Navy for thirty-six years. As a schoolboy he trained at the Royal Naval College in Dartmouth before going to sea as a midshipman at the age of seventeen. At twenty-five, he took command of his first ship, the destroyer *HMS Brissendon*. Other destroyers or frigates he commanded were *HMS Comus, HMS Cossack* and *HMS Dido*. His last appointment was as Commodore in Charge in Hong Kong, where he remained for two years.

Roger retired from the navy in 1973. In 1976 he was elected chairman of the Waveney District Council. He also served as a Yarmouth port and haven commissioner, a member of the Local Review Committee at Blundeston Prison, secretary of Wissett Parochial Church Council, president of the Aldeburgh branch of the Royal Naval Association among other commitments during his distinguished career and retirement. Katharine has been secretary of the Aldeburgh RNA, and with Roger worked seven acres of land, to the contentment of their donkeys, dogs and cats. They returned the house to its pre-Victorian state with the help of Billy and John Thompson - 'a whole year's work.' Everyone mourned the recent death of Roger, in the autumn of the year 2000.

*Wissett Fête Fancy Dress line-up, c1975. Left to right, standing: Maureen Hunt, Angela Reeder, Sadie Wing, Robert Oddy, Stephen Oddy, Katharine Wykes-Sneyd, Dorothy Kiddy. Sitting: Sally Reeder and Patrick Wing.*

19

## Rickyards

Mrs Meek sold to the Kiddy family the Whitehouse Farm stackyard, which is where this bungalow was built in 1976 for Albert and Dorothy Kiddy on their retirement from Wissett Lodge.

Mrs Daphne Ritchie has a hilarious recollection of her husband Bill at Rickyards. The occasion was the Queen's Silver Jubilee in 1977: the whole village had been invited by Albert and Dorothy to a barbecue. Entertainment was laid on, and during a gap in the jollities, Bill said, 'All right, I'll give you a turn!' He jumped up onto the raised bank that acted as a dais, and in his kilt, performing a bit of a sword-dance, he sang 'Daisy, Daisy! Give me your answer do!' in Urdu.

Brian and Patricia Adams live at Rickyards now, having bought it from Norman and Mary Johnson in 1989. They moved in permanently in June 1998 after retiring, and have extended the premises three times.

## Tudor Cottage

This beautifully restored old house used to have another wing which is believed to date from 1483. The remaining wing dates from the late sixteenth century.

By 1840, it comprised thirty-four acres and, as part of the Ash Tree Farm estate, was owned by John Arnott Esq and managed by Allington Carman as a double dwelling. According to the 1881 census, it housed 'Morriss Jessop, threshing machine attendant and engine driver,' his wife Alice, and their four-year-old daughter Eliza, all relatives of the Jessops at Ash Tree Farm. At the beginning of the 1900s, the whole estate was owned by Herbert Broom, along with his other assets. In all probability, it was he who demolished one wing of Tudor Cottage and used the materials to revamp and enlarge Ash tree Farm.

By then Herbert Moore lived in one half of the cottage, as groom to the farm horses (Suffolk Punches). His daughter Hazel (now Hazel Hunt) was born here. Mr Alfred Barber lived in the other side, and was groom to the race horses that Lewis Parry trained and rode. A Mr 'Digger' Warne is also thought to have lived here at some time, and worked on the estate.

When Mr Sawyer took over Ash Tree farm and Tudor Cottage, his estate hand Harry Edwards lived with his wife in Tudor Cottage. It has been rumoured that Mr Sawyer promised to leave Harry the cottage plus £1000 when he died; but when that time came, he had deducted a nought, so Harry received the cottage and £100, not £1000! After Harry's death in 1956, his son Billy and wife Ellen remained at the cottage. Then Billy ('the dustman') died at only fifty-eight in 1971, followed by his mother Ellen in 1973. So the cottage was left to Billy's sister Lillian who lived at The Elms, Walpole, with her husband Andy Saunders. Lillian sold in 1974 to Neil Alleston Lanham who briefly owned Tudor Cottage before it was sold to Andrew Lissak and Monica Knight.

In 1978, the cottage, now in a derelict state, was bought by the visionary Alan Manton and his wife Julia. Local farmers remember Mr Manton, an architect, going over to

*Tudor Cottage in the 1930s*

Haughley timber-yard near Stowmarket to select huge green oak trunks and driving them with great effort back to Wissett on his trailer-tractor, in order to re-build Tudor Cottage and restore it to its sixteenth-century status. This was the start of what was to become a twelve-year project.

Firstly, the main frame timbers had to be preserved. Alan numbered all the savable beams, one by one, and collected all the reusable wattle and daub. Between the main frame posts were fixed narrow panels of hazel rods, the 'wattle.' This wattle was then daubed with vatsful of clay lump mixed with straw, manure and horsehair that had been squelched into a sticky mess (ie the 'daub'). The daubed areas were then plastered over and persuaded to adhere in position by liberal pokings with dibblers! Mike Fordham and family who lived nearby helped with the daubing.

This ambitious regeneration of Tudor Cottage was finalized by the Hendersons.

## Ash Tree Farm

This modest farmhouse was named after the two ash trees at the road end of the original straight drive. The trees are still visible in the present hedge. The place was owned in the 1830 to 40s by John Arnott and occupied by Allington Carman. By 1881, Harriet Jessop, widow of John Jessop, farmer, had travelled from Wyverstone (near Stowmarket) to farm Ash Tree's seventy acres, with only one farmhand and her eighteen-year-old son Harry, and four younger children: Elizabeth, John, Harriet and Florence. A decade later, the farm was home to George Tyrrell, his wife Berthelina and their four daughters: Florence, Alice, May and Edith. In the early 1900s, the place was bought by Herbert Broom, and in 1910, it became the home of the newly-wedded Joy Stanford and her husband Lewis Henry Parry. Both families were well-connected, the Stanfords being partners with Herbert Broom in real estate in the Halesworth area, and Lewis being the son of James Parry, maltster, who built the maltings complex by Halesworth railway station, and the brother of Major Richard Allen Parry, DSO, who came to live at Ash Tree after the Great War. Major Parry had been Captain of the F Company of the 4th Battalion Suffolk Regiment from 1901-1912. During World War I he went to France with the 4th Suffolks and was wounded in 1915, and bravely brought in some of his wounded men while under fire.

Ash Tree Farm was enlarged, thatched, and timbered, probably by Stanford/Broom. Lewis and his brother ran the family business and bred horses. In 1929, Lewis rode in the Grand National his horse called Kilbairn, which he trained himself. They finished ninth out of sixty-six starters. Apparently Kilbairn's name can still be deciphered over one of the stable doors, and the name of his blood-brother, Silbane, over one of the others. For daily exercise, Kilbairn and Silbane raced against each other up and down the 'one mile stretch,' supposedly the full length of Mill Road. Lewis had owned another horse that subsequently achieved fame in the Grand National: Peter The Piper. Lewis also rode in steeple-chases, and was one of the best point-to-point trainers.

Joy and Lewis's son David was born in 1931. Mrs Sadd (from Stone Cottage), who wheeled him round in his pram, proudly used to say that the first words David uttered were, 'Mrs Sadd! Mrs Sadd!' Shortly afterwards, the Parrys moved to Hooker House in Halesworth and Mr and Mrs Sawyer moved in to Ash Tree. The Sawyers sold to Peter and Lettice Lambert, who moved in on the last day of the war in 1945. A pilot who crash-landed in the stream below the garden in 1945 was rescued by Mrs Lambert. Peter Lambert had been awarded the Military Cross for his bravery at Ypres in the First World War.

The Lamberts' son, Miles, lived at Ash Tree Farm with his wife Armorel until 1995. Their great interests are antiques and collectables. Their shop, Occasions, is in Halesworth Thoroughfare, and the Halesworth Antiques Street Market is their brainchild.

The present owner of Ash Tree Farm is Dieter Stiele.

## The Drift

It would be hard to visualize this tranquil, spacious bungalow, set on grassy orchard slopes next to Ash Tree Farm as it first was in 1955 or so.

Miles Lambert had it erected for his gardener, Mr Janes. Subsequently, the bungalow was snugly bricked round for Miles' mother to move there in 1978.

The present owner, Hugh Barrett, is a writer. His first book, about an apprenticeship to a Suffolk farmer, *Early to Rise - A Suffolk Morning* (1967), is widely acclaimed as a classic of its kind, in the tradition of Adrian Bell's *Corduroy* or John Stewart Collis' *The Worm Forgives The Plough*.

Hugh initially broadcast his own work on the BBC Radio's 'Farm Fare' series in 1953. After two weeks, taking over from AG Street, he became Chairman of this feature, that was broadcast at noon on Wednesdays. Hugh went on to present television programmes ('.......black and white, of course, then.') and he remained a familiar voice on the radio, not only on farming programmes, but schools broadcasting and the overseas service.

*A Good Living*, Hugh's latest book, published in the year 2000, has been written entirely in Wissett. It is an autobiographical sequel to *Early to Rise* and as Ronald Blythe writes in the Introduction, the author 'combines earthiness with vision.'

*Book jacket, 'Early to Rise.' A new edition is due in the summer of 2001.*

## Nos 1 to 6 Farm Close

Cynthia Nunn writes that she and her husband Derek developed the Farm Close site, and that one of their daughters, Alice, built No 4 house in 1998. Having returned from her travels round Australia, Alice is currently teaching at a special school.

There will be a total of six houses in all. At No 6 are Chris and Karen Calver, who had their house built while living in a caravan on site. They only recently moved in and are busy with the finishing touches. The son of Ray and Angie Calver of St Peter's Farm Bungalow, Wissett, Chris works for British Telecom, whilst Karen works for The Norwich Union Building Society. No 5 is still not completed but is being built by Roger Foster from Halesworth. No 3 is owned by Kevin and Claire Parry, who came from Somerset via Halesworth. Their two children are Samuel (6) and Sophie (3). Kevin works at Sizewell nuclear power station. No 2 is completed, while No 1 has its foundations laid.

*Wissett Football Team 1930-31: Back Row - Walter Kerrison, Dick Foster, Frank Crane, Billy Aldred, 'Juggler' Wright, Neddy Bacon, Billy Thompson senior. Front Row - 'Puff' Seaman, Bob Kent, ?, Hector Calver, Herbie Bacon, Billy Thompson junior, George Bacon, Bert Aldred.*

## Bond's Farm

This farm was managed by Robert Aldred for William Pattison in the 1830s and 40s, according to the old Tithe lists. By 1892, it was owned by George Veasy, then between 1896 and 1900 by George Tyrrell, who owned Ash Tree Farm too. Tales are still told of Pilfer Chapman, who regularly stole from his ever-tolerant master, Mr Tyrrell. There were many comings and goings during the twentieth century: by 1916, Mrs Laura Moore had retired to the farm, which was then run by her sons. William Gale owned Bond's briefly around 1922-23; then Rosetta Frost, daughter of the miller AS Calver, held the property until 1933, when it passed to her husband, Arthur Frost. The Frosts moved to Corner Farm, and let Bond's Farm to several different people. A Mrs Stannard was one such lessee. She had been left with a small orphaned boy. When her lease at Bond's was up, she begged

Nellie Oxborough (then at St Peter's Farm Cottage) to care for the child. That little boy was Cyril Maulden, and it was Nellie and Freddie Oxborough who brought him up.

Another tenant at Bond's was Cecil Bunbury, son of George Henry Bunbury who had built Willow Grange. He arrived with his heavily pregnant wife, Lillie, who was spotted walking down Wissett Street and targeted as a future employer by the aspiring nursery-maids in the village. Elizabeth Taylor, about fourteen at the time, was chosen by Lillie to help with the new-born babe. One of Elizabeth's tasks was to take the curly-haired little Jolyon for walks in his pram. She'd trundle him along to Saffron Cottage, where Ted Cutts, who loved children (having six of his own), would offer Jolyon cake. 'Cakie! Cakie!' the little fellow would call. But one day, the cake had currants in. Subsequently, Lillie found the currants in the contents of her son's pottie, to her horror. Jolyon remained incorrigibly healthy. On one unforgettable occasion, Lillie told Elizabeth that she was going to be away for the day, 'but you can come up just the same, and Cecil will take Jolyon out.' Cecil did so, but arrived home in the late afternoon a little worse for wear. 'I've had a little accident,' he confessed. When Elizabeth went to look at the baby, she found him with blood all over the pram pillow and scratches scoring his face. Mercifully he was asleep. 'Poor little old Humpty Dumpty!' murmured Cecil in a haze. While Elizabeth woke the child and cleaned him up, it transpired that his father had broken their walk by stopping off at an untold number of 'watering places' and accidentally tipped Jolyon out of his pram.

The Frosts sold the farm in 1939 to Cyril Colbeck, but it was only a few months before Mr Colbeck sold to Jane and Charles Wiseman, on 27 January 1940. Within another few months, the farm was sold again: to Amy and John De Quincey, on 3 May 1940.

*Wissett Football Team 1931-32: Back Row - 'Puff' Seaman, Frank Crane, Walter Crane, Neddie Bacon, Dick Foster, Bert Aldred. Middle Row - George Rose, Bob Kent, Fred Read. Front Row - Reggie Barber, Billy Aldred, Jack Saunders, Billy Thompson, Peter Gee.*

The De Quinceys stayed until 1946; they owned the first tractor-combine.

Next to arrive at the farm was Maurice Fuller, who stayed for two years, followed by Henry and Elizabeth Merryweather, then Frederick and Kate Neate. Each of the last two couples stayed for a year and a half or less. William Holden took over on the 4 August 1950, and remained for ten years before selling to Richard Willis.

Mr Willis came from Essex, and hand-milked his herd of Jersey cows. His family and local archaeologists found many Roman potsherds and evidence of a thriving Roman settlement on the southern slopes of the fields. In the early 1970s, Mr Willis gifted an acre of land to his son, Tony, and on retirement, another six. The rest of the farm was sold to Ron and Jean Nightingale, who in turn sold to Cynthia and Derek Nunn in 1988. Cynthia and Derek used to run the Post Office and shop at St Cross, and have become very much part of Wissett. Their delicious strawberries will be remembered by many; they were eaten in abundance at the Treacle Fairs. Derek has a fruit and vegetable shop in Bungay and Cynthia had one in Halesworth (Melons) until recently. Derek is a parish councillor and is always willing to help anyone, being very generous with his time, and his produce.

## Thyme Cottage

Patricia Willis recounts: 'We started building Thyme Cottage in 1972, after drawing up the plans ourselves. Tony's father gave us just under an acre of land behind Bond's Farm known as Back Paddock.

'We used second-hand materials where possible, partly to try and give the appearance of an old building to blend in with the surroundings, but also for economic reasons. Recycled bricks were very much cheaper in the early seventies!

'The bricks in the chimney and west end wall were from a demolished farm building in Debenham; the south-facing front wall from a farmhouse in Cratfield and the back wall and east wall from old stables at St Michael's South Elmham. These bricks had been made at the old St Cross brickworks and they have the '+' trademark imprinted in the 'frogs.' They were given to us providing we dismantled the building ourselves. Bricks laid in days gone by are reasonably easy to clean because the builders used lime mortar instead of cement. All the bricks are old Suffolk reds, but there is a slight variation in colour and texture depending on where they were made.

'We always thought it seemed a shame that all the decorative crosses should be hidden inside the walls so we used some of them with the 'frogs' exposed, in the fireplace and along the top of an inside wall. The large oak beam over the fireplace was once the cornerpost of an ancient barn, and the Gothic-shaped back door came from St Peter's Church, Lowestoft.

'A local builder did the main brickwork on Thyme Cottage after we had completed the foundations. We managed to put the roof on with some expert help. The timbers had to be new wood according to regulations, but we used old red pantiles.

'The building was completed and we moved in, in November 1976.'
Patricia Willis                                                                                        March 2000

As well as Greenpeace, Patricia and Tony actively support the Suffolk Wildlife Trust.

They are re-planting withy beds for basket-making, which is one of Tony's skills. Patricia has devoted her life to providing natural habitats on her land for a wide variety of flora and fauna. She has a number of 'retired' animals that she tends, including two Jacob's horned ewes, a Texel sheep, and four speckle-faced Beulah Welsh sheep, that Suffolk Wildlife had commissioned originally to be transported from Wales to graze the Suffolk heathlands and keep down the silver birch saplings. As well as the sheep, Patricia and Tony have given over several of their paddocks as retirement homes to a Vietnamese pig, an elderly nanny-goat, a hen-pecked cockerel and various fowl.

## Brickhill Cottages

These twelve houses stretch in a row from No 1 at the Halesworth end of Wissett Street to No 12 nearest the centre of the village. The first numbers, 1 - 4, were pre-war, and 5 - 12 were built just after the war, as part of the council's re-housing project. A number of the houses are now privately owned.

So many tenants have moved in and out of these houses that unfortunately they can't all be enumerated.

## Nos 1 to 4 Brickhill Cottages

These cottages were built in the early 1930s, at a cost of £450 a pair.
Elizabeth Davey can remember the builder letting her lay two of the first bricks of No 1 while it was being built, and people can distantly remember the first tenant as Alan Cutts, oldest son of Edward ('Poodle') Cutts. Poodle and his wife Alice retired here from Stone Cottage and were joined by some of their younger children too. Alan, a Halesworth maltster, and his wife Agnes remained here after Poodle and Alice had gone. The next inhabitant was Jimmy Laws, who was employed by the Meeks at Whitehouse Farm.

Jacqueline and Robert Kimber own this cottage now, and live here with their children: Dale, Mark, Paul, Cara and Aaron.

The Meens lived for a while at No 2. Jimmy and Edith Meen moved from what was Little Hill House (now Tarleton) in 1931 with their four children: Roland, Kenneth, Donald and Betty. Roland (Roly) remembers arriving here when he was eleven; it was the first time that they didn't have to get water from the pond. There was a hand pump behind Nos 2 and 3. Jimmy was an agricultural worker for Mr Lewis Rowe at Valley Farm and Mrs Meen used to do the washing for Mrs Craddock at The Pines (now Hill Farm).

Roly lost a leg in a railway accident during the war but went on to work for Mr Richardson at The Pines. Donald worked at Manor Farm and Kenneth went into the navy. Roly remembers 'visiting' The Swan and how he could throw a 'crafty' dart. If you won, you would get a free half pint, and at one time, Roly had a table full of half pints! Roly married in 1945 and moved to Halesworth.

In 1934 or 35, Shilly Mouser moved here from Church Cottages after his wife died, with his son Freddie and a housekeeper. Among those who lived here after the Mousers were Sidney Moore and family.

One of the more recent tenants at No 2 was Mr Philip Rees, who now runs his antique shop in Lowestoft. He used to be road-manager for the pop group The Who, and has countless escapades to relate about Keith Moon and the rest. The present incumbents are Karin and Maurice Hawkins, aptly named, since Maurice is a falconer. With their children, Glen and Ashley, they came from Romney Marsh in 1995.

The clearest early memory of No 3 is of the Laws family. Walter, one of Mr Meek's cowmen at Whitehouse Farm, and Bertha his wife were here from 1943 to the mid 1950s with their children: David, Allen, Reg and Walter. Young Allen also worked for Mr Meek but was only fifteen when he died of what was thought to be peritonitis. Walter Laws junior was the torpedo operator in a World War II submarine and, shockingly, was killed on duty. David was in the navy at eighteen and travelled all over the Mediterranean. He married Gwyneth Newby in the 1950s and moved to Halesworth. David was very involved in the Wissett Football Club which he helped to run from 1947 to 1950. He started as the linesman and then the referee and became Secretary at the finish. Walter died in the 1950s and his wife moved to Homersfield.

Jacqueline and Eric Andrews were next to live at No 3. Jackie is Cyril Maulden's daughter. Then Howell Wing and his wife Jean (daughter of Madge Cutts) arrived with their children: Teresa, Sadie, Maria, Patrick and Glen. They came from near Blyford and stayed until 1973 when they moved down the road to No 9 Brickhill Cottage. After the Wings were Frank and Vera Blowers, who both worked for Captain Chute at Bulhams Covert. Today the occupants of No 3 are Edwin (Eddie) Spooner, his daughter Sarah and son Brent.

Memories of No 4 stretch back to 1945, when the inhabitants were Robert Fleming (Beryl McMorran's grandfather) and Ellen Francis the housekeeper. In 1956, Ivy Block moved

*Wissett Football Team c1950: Back Row - Bill Goddard, John Boast, Dick Fenn, Bob Smith, Keith Somerfield, Charlie Mower. Front Row - Peter Cutts, Fred Robson, Sidney Rayner, Stanley Dossett, Peter Etheridge.*

into this house as the newly-wed Mrs Cullingford. With her husband Herbert, she looked after her father, Billy Block. In 1974, Beryl and Andrew (Andy) McMorran moved in, taking over from Beryl's aunt Ivy, who moved to Bramfield. Beryl and Andy's children grew up in this house: Debbie, having trained in nursing, works at the Norfolk and Norwich Hospital as a Theatre Nurse. Her brother Stuart is at Lincoln University studying Graphic Design. Andy spent many years on gas-rigs off the coast at Yarmouth, and can turn his hand to most things in the way of building and gardening, trimming and tidying, including the former playing field in Buntings Lane, and the churchyard. Beryl is renowned for her catering skills and her ability to arrange and decorate, and support village fund-raising fairs in a thousand and one ways.

## Nos 5 to 12 Brickhill Cottages

These cottages were built in 1947.

Harry Copping and his mother lived at No 5 immediately after it was built. Harry was short of stature but always laughing. He worked for Mrs Eastcott as the cowman at Red House Farm. He was notorious for 'smoking like a chimney.' After Harry, the Flint family arrived. Bridget is still here with four of her seven children, who, in descending order are: Nokomis, Luke, Jason, Matthew, Simon, Michael and Robert.

Into the newly-built No 6 came Peter Cutts and his wife Glenna. As the youngest son of Poodle and Alice, Peter has spent all his life in Wissett. Although born in Stone Cottage, he grew up in No 1 Brickhill Cottage. It was at No 6 that Glenna and Peter brought up their children, Linda and Malcolm. Glenna enjoyed the outdoor life, mainly in the fruit fields, working for Mr and Mrs Richardson and then for Martin Kempe picking apples. Her presence is sorely missed since her death in 1993. Peter has spent all his working life, forty-five years so far, working in the Wissett orchards, firstly for Don

*Wissett Football Team c1970: Back Row - Peter Cutts, Henry Williams, Harry Leggett, Brian Warne, Alistair Tomkins, John Thompson, John Reeder, Kenny Barnard, Katharine Wykes-Sneyed, Billy Thompson, John Hall. Front Row - Trevor Calver, Peter Fleming, Malcom Cutts, Colin Whistlecraft, Brian Felgate, Keith Townsend.*

Meen at Manor Farm, then for Mr Richardson at The Pines and again for Martin Kempe until Manor Farm was sold. There is virtually nothing Peter does not know about plants and horticulture. He has exhibited successfully on numerous occasions at Wissett Horticultural Show. Moreover, Peter has been a keen fisherman and sportsman. As a young man, he was a member of the Wissett Football Club from 1947 until it folded three years later. According to David Laws, Peter was a 'fast little winger.' Another pastime of Peter's is bowling: he has been a member of the Bowls Club from the beginning.

When No 7 was brand-new, Charlie Fleming and his wife Lily (née Block) moved here from Hall Farm (now Oaklands). Their daughter Beryl, then five, and her two brothers, Billy and Peter, went to the Wissett school until it closed in 1961.

After Charlie died, Lily took her brother Leonard Block in, until he also died. After the Flemings, a Terry Rivet lived here, followed by Fred and Mary Shadbolt. The present occupants are Harry Cross and his partner, Marg. Between them, they have had six children and twice as many bicycles to-ing and fro-ing in their household. Marg is an inspired craftswoman, particularly in rug-making and soft furnishing. Her work can be seen in certain arts and crafts centres in Bungay. Harry tackles anything electrical and rises to most challenges, especially if they involve cross-country cycling or animal welfare.

The original occupant of No 8 was 'Old Mr Mann,' pigman for Captain Chute at Bulhams. Rozlyn and John Hall (son of Mrs Hall in No 11) lived here next, for several years bringing up their four children, James, Eric, Ivan and Zena. After them, two Taylor families lived here: first Johnny and Pauline Taylor with three children, then the second Taylor influx. Now No 8 is the home of the Mills family: Helen, Brian, Darren and Tony.

Memories are a little patchy as to the earlier inhabitants of No 9. Villagers today recall rather vaguely a number of names - Mr Kenny, Mrs Saxby and daughter Kathleen, Lenny Dickerson and wife Freda, Mrs Neeve......

Members of the Wing family have lived here since 1973, when Jean and Howell Wing and children arrived from No 3. Howell worked for Anglian Drainage, while Jean did seasonal apple picking for Mr Kempe at Manor Farm and strawberry picking for Hector Calver. Jean died two or three years ago, all too young. Of the five children, Sadie and Teresa have married and moved away. Sadie has fond memories of growing up in Wissett: playing at Jimmy Cutts' place, lobbing balls on Colonel and Mrs Tomkin's tennis courts at The Red House during the summer holidays, or being floated down the Beck in a pram by Maureen Hunt and her sister Teresa when the pram sank. Maria, the third sister, has moved in with her partner Mark Hurren; both are new and proud parents of baby Harvey. Glen Wing continues to live at No 9, now joined by his girlfriend Julia Chatten-Berry .

Reggie and Evelyn Darch lived at No 10 from when it was new. Reggie worked at a Chediston fruit farm. The couple had two daughters: Sandra and Verlene. Today John Catchpole lives here with his partner Veronica Emery, and one of Veronica's five children, Julian. The Emerys came to Wissett after spending several years in Australia, and for a while had the cramped excitement of lodging in a caravan behind The Plough Inn until a house became available. John is widely respected as an excellent builder, and throughout the summer of 2000 was to be found working late on a Friday evening in the churchyard with Julian Harris and other dedicated 'movers,' heaving away rubble and ancient

Nellie Hall and grandchildren

undergrowth from the tombs before getting on with the back-breaking work of clearing the high grass and throttling ivy so as to restore the churchyard to its former well-trimmed tranquillity.

At No 11 lived Mrs Nellie Hall and four of her children, Doreen, Mollie, Edna and Alan. They originally had come to Rumburgh as evacuees from London. Nellie's husband had been run over by a bus and killed during the Blitz. Unfortunately Mrs Hall's older son, John, for reasons of housing, had to stay in Rumburgh when the others moved to Wissett. Mollie married a Rumburgh man and emigrated to New Zealand, followed there by Doreen. Edna is now in Kent, while the brothers have stayed in Suffolk: Alan and his wife Christine are in nearby Holton, having brought up two children, Caroline and Brian. John, with his family grown up, lives near Saxmundham.

Trevor Pearce and Janice Bathgate live at No 11 now. Trevor's wife was Annette, the daughter of William Bird who lived up the Mill Road. Their daughter, Amanda, married a year or two ago.

The first to live in house No 12 were Jimmy and Harold ('Fella') Cutts with their widowed sister Madge Kent and her three children: Jean (later Jean Wing), Michael and Megan. After Madge's second marriage to Billy Woolner, the pair moved into The Plough Inn, as landlords. Fella and Jimmy were gone, and. Basil and Lily Hambling moved here from No 13. Various people came and went, and this cottage had had a rather turbulent past by the time the Kimbers were here. They felt it was possessed by a poltergeist. However, the place has been 'cleansed' and the present owners, Frances and Alasdair Campbell, have experienced no strange happenings. Francis and Alasdair came from Bungay in 1996 with their two children: Laura who is thirteen and James, ten. Alasdair is a building consultant and Frances assists Trevor at The Plough Inn.

31

## Nos 13 and 14 Brickhill Bungalows

These two bungalows were built in about 1952 and the first tenants in No 13 were Basil and Lily Hambling. Basil had grown up at Hawes (Hors) Farm with his parents John and Ethel Hambling. Next to reside in this bungalow were Mr and Mrs Needham with their two sons, followed by Jimmy and Helen Nunn, who moved from Halleluia Cottage in 1964.

The present occupant is Reginald Brown. Reg moved here from Westhall, with his elderly mother, in the 1970s. He is a farm implement enthusiast and has been for many years involved in the maintenance and repairing of farm machinery. He reminisces over the 'cocoa-tin' Massey Fergusson combine: so nick-named because there was no hatch access on the top to get down into the machine, and yet the metal was so thin that 'you could open it with a jack-knife or tin-opener, like you would open a cocoa-tin' to get down the back of the 'shakers.' Reg is a committee member of the annual Henham Steam Rally, and a steward of the vintage Tractor Run starting at the Henham Estate. He has worked at most of the farms in the area with thrashing contractors. Reg's sister Lilian and her friend May Mahoney were maids to Mrs Eagle Bott and her daughters, Lizzie and Beatrice, while they lived at Holton Mill. Reg remembers Mrs Eagle Bott as a tiny lady in black dresses with lace collars.

In No 14 live Harold Leggett and Peggy Stokes. Harold has been here since the bungalow was built in 1952, having come from Homersfield. Before retiring, he was at Halesworth United Dairies, then at Howard Rotavators where he worked on the famous 'nut' for the old Lowestoft swing bridge. Then Harold was a long-distance lorry-driver, and finally a driver for Fibrenyle of Beccles. He was a keen member of the Wissett football team and appears in several of the old village team photos. David Laws remembers Harold as the best goal keeper. Peggy has lived here since 1981, having come from Bungay.

*Old steam-roller and men at work tarmacking the road.*

## No 1 The Street

Before Mr William Thompson built his bungalow on this site, it used to be called Godbold's meadow and belonged to Whitehouse Farm.

Two ladies, now in their late seventies, remember a very odd occurrence over this meadow in April 1925. The ladies were then very small girls, Madge Cutts and Elizabeth Taylor, being taken for their Sunday afternoon walk by Madge's father, Mr Ted Cutts. As was his wont on a Sunday, Ted was wearing his trilby and swinging his walking stick. Suddenly he looked up and told the girls to do likewise. What they saw was a giant airship with R33 written on its flank. 'It's the Pulham Pig!' went the cry round the village. High in the sky, it gradually floated towards Halesworth, and disappeared. It transpired that the Pig (named after its shape) had been out on a series of experiments from its 'shed' at Pulham airfield.

In 1935 or 36, William Thompson ('Billy' to everyone in the village) bought the meadow and built the bungalow here. He reminisces over his long life:

'I was born in Framsden, where my father was the local Police Constable. The police had to live in married quarters then. We moved to Worlingworth, where my younger sister was born. The pattern was to stay seven or eight years in one house then move on. We went to Blythburgh, then in 1920s (I must have been about fifteen) we came to Wissett, where Father finished up his time. We lived in the house next to the school.

'I would like to have been a detective, but I followed the trade of carpenter and joiner. I built this bungalow on the site of Wissett rifle-range and quoits ground. I married Joyce in 1936, having finished building our home.'

*Wissett Football Committee 1951-52: Back Row - Ray Stebbings, Stanley Abbott, Dick Foster. Front Row - ?, Billy Thompson, Fred Read, Henry Aldred.*

Billy was an enthusiastic member of the Football Club, and managed it for some years. He followed other sports keenly: village cricket, bowls and rifle matches. He helped his son John build 'Woodville.' He was an agent for Tilley lamps and radiators, and ladies who were in service at Wissett Lodge in the 1930s describe the Tilley lamps that 'were in every room' at The Lodge.

Joyce and Billy have witnessed a number of natural phenomena during their life in the village. Not only do they recall the earth tremor of 1931, but the 'really wonderful sight' of the northern lights, the aurora borealis, in the night sky of 25 January 1938. The 'Rory Bory Alice' was the talk in The Plough for quite a while; it has been seen in this area of Suffolk more frequently than might be supposed.

Dramas not only of earth and sky, but of water too have been experienced in Wissett. Joyce remembers especially the Great Flood of September 1968 when the Beck became a raging torrent and swept a carful of people into a low brick wall next to the post office. Fortunately the driver and four passengers survived.

Joyce has been a devoted housewife and mother, involved in many of the village activities. She can remember the days when the chapel next door was filled with singing and worshippers coming in by the busload from Halesworth on the occasion of religious festivals such as Whitsun. She even recalls the little hand-mower she used to cut the two front areas of grass that sloped up to the chapel porch. Joyce has won many trophies for flower-arranging, and is a charming painter in oils of Suffolk scenes.

## Brambleside

To build this bungalow 'up Buntkins' (Buntings Lane), Mrs Dora Warren bought a plot of land from Mr Meek of Whitehouse Farm. It was on an ancient sand pit that might have been part of the site of a Roman settlement. Further up the hill was an old clay pit. The Romans preferred sand to build their villas on; in Wissett, the lower south-facing slopes of what is now Bond's Farm were ideal.

Dora is one of the three daughters of Annie Taylor (née Oxborough), and the mother of Patricia Willis at nearby Thyme Cottage. Dora has a lifelong loyalty to Wissett, having spent her whole life here, as indeed have many other residents.

## Woodville

John Thompson built this bungalow with his father's help in 1974. John grew up in Wissett, at No 1 The Street just down the lane, with his parents Billy and Joyce. John is a carpenter, like his father, while Anne, his wife, has worked in the jeweller's shop in Halesworth. They have a son Jonathan who is ten. John has been a keen footballer and he too can be seen on some of the old village football team photos. These days John enjoys running and has run the London Marathon a couple of times for charity.

*General Note on all the Property from Buntings Lane westwards to No 19 The Street.*

From contracts, schedules and abstracts of titles dating from 1812, it is evident that Anthony Barber owned the 5¼ acre 'Allotment field' - still clearly visible on modern OS maps - and all the property edging it, from the site of The Old Chapel through to No 19 The Street. Barber kept the rectangular site of Nos 18 and 19 The Street; but after various wheelings and dealings involving mortgages to a Reverend Jeremy Day (1820) and to the three Wales sisters, Lydia, Ann and Susan (1832), Barber conveyed the rest of the land and properties in May 1835 to the miller, Samuel Farrow, and the manager of Wissett Hall and owner of Broadway Farm, Jonathan Howlett. By October of the same year, the properties were 'assigned' to John Phillips, the newcomer from London, and his heirs.

By 'reciting' Phillips' will and studying the 1839-41 Tithe map one can surmise how John Phillips operated without having to pay any tithes. Initially, the buildings on his land, from east to west, were these: three separate dwellings on the site of cottages now known as Nos 2 - 7 The Street; the 'brewhouse' with its shop, stable, outbuildings and yards (The Plough); 'three tenements or cottages' adjoining the brewhouse, on the site of what are now Nos 9 and 10 The Street; a 'double tenement or cottage' where now No 12 stands; and 'five several tenements or cottages' (Nos 13 - 17 The Street). The Tithe map may be inaccurate, in that Phillips may have developed the cottages which are now Nos 2 - 7 into two terraces of three and four cottages each before the final date of the Tithe record: 1841.

What is certain is that Phillips and his business associates raised a mortgage for £600 in April 1841, and that he presented the Protestant Dissenters of Halesworth Society with the easternmost bottom corner of his land for the building of the Wissett chapel, and also

donated £100 for the same cause. He conveyed the title deeds to the chapel trustees in December 1841.

Before his death in 1846, Phillips had paid off all his debts, sold the plot on which cottages No 2 - 7 stand to Charles Borrows, and appointed trustees for all his remaining Wissett land. No doubt he had land elsewhere; his wife Eve was sister to Stephen Wright of Bramfield, and two of her relatives (Henry Lock and Samuel Wright Lock) later became trustees to John Phillips' Wissett property, after the first trustees, Robert Aldred, William George and William Lincolne had died or resigned. Phillips' chief beneficiaries of his Wissett premises and 'messuages' were his cousin Thomas Carman, and the children of Anthony and Susan Button of Bramfield. Two of these children were

*The Old Chapel interior*

named after the Phillips: a son, Phillips (including the 's'), and Lucy Eve, one of the daughters. This son, young Phillips John Button, died in 1866, before reaching twenty-one, so he was unable to inherit his share; the other son, Charles John Button, sold his share in 1878 to his three sisters: Emma (now married to Samuel Dolling of Loughborough); Eliza, who lived in Middlesex; and Lucy Eve, who resided in Clifton, Bristol.

Forty-five years after the death of John Phillips, and after several loans, deaths, disclaimers and an emigration, the Phillips properties in Wissett were divided into lots and 'on Tuesday, 22nd September, 1891, at 4 o'clock to the minute in the afternoon' put up for auction at the Angel Hotel, Halesworth, under the hammer of Messrs Lenny, Smith & Stanford. Lot 1 was The Plough, with its detached flour house and wash-house, outhouses and 'piggeries'; Lot 2 was the 'double cottage' which until at least 1882 had been 'three tenements' (now Nos 9 and 10 The Street); Lot 3 was the 'double tenement' (now No 12); Lot 4 was the terrace of 'five several tenements or cottages,' Nos 13 to 17 The Street.

# The Old Chapel

The day that Wissett chapel was opened for public worship has been immortalized in the words of Mr Charles Haward, one of the Halesworth chapel deacons:

'I had the happiness to unite with a goodly company assembled there. That gathering on the noted 27th October 1841 was worthy of remembrance. As the day went on there was a drenching rain. A spread in a tent near Mr Aldred's house (Whitehouse Farm) hard by, from the heavy downpour, was not pleasant to reach, and the water in places dropping through, did not increase the enjoyment of the party. Leaving the village after the day's services, for a full quarter of a mile along the road foot passengers could only travel by wading through the stream, at a greater or less depth.' Charles Haward then notes that his sister-in-law, Miss Bayley, wrote some commemorative verses which she termed the 'Wissetation.'

William Lincolne, one of the trustees, noted the day in his diary: 'Oct 27th, opening of the small Chapel at Wissett. Mr Sprigg, of Ipswich, preached, and a tea meeting held in a booth erected for the purpose on the premises of our friend Aldred. The weather was very unfavourable, had it been held the day following the meeting must have been given up, the floods were so heavy.'

Mr and Mrs Phillips, the benefactors of Wissett chapel, had been members of the Halesworth Independent meeting house since 1838. They are both interred in Wissett chapel enclosure.

Amongst the first trustees, as well as the wealthy drapers and hemp merchants: William Lincolne, James and Robert Aldred, and Jonathan Corbyn, were the Reverend George Larkworthy Smith, a Halesworth chapel minister; Samuel Roper, a Halesworth bookseller; and John London, a Halesworth hatter. Others from the farming community were: William George of Halesworth; Robert Haward Crisp of Wissett; Jonathan Corbyn

*The Old Chapel c1930 (inspired by a drawing by Arnold Beverley)*

Bishop of Chediston; and John Gibbon Thompson of Blyford. The Haward family, many of whom lived in Wissett, were also represented by Robert Haward, 'Gentleman' of Bramfield.

Services were held on Sundays and during the week, those on the Sabbath being conducted by local preachers. A favourite with the congregation was Mr J Bird, the Methodist grandfather of Miss Hannah Bird of Wissett, who travelled the district for over fifty years conducting services. Others devoted to the Wissett chapel were Mr Joseph Bishop, who lived at Valley Farm, and one of his sons, William Bishop, who became the first superintendent of the Sunday School, which was started in 1887. William Bishop had six children, whose initials can be discerned on some of the bricks of the chapel extension built in 1882. Joseph Bishop gave his six grandchildren two shillings each to lay the bricks. The extension was in the form of a new classroom and vestry, at a total cost of £62.

The Sunday School flourished about this period with nearly a hundred children. In subsequent years the numbers slowly dropped and dwindled to eighteen in 1916, in which year the School had to close. Miss H Bird, Mr Arthur Kemp and Miss Allen were among the teachers. The Wissett children always shared in a summer treat with the Halesworth Sunday School. The Wissett contingent was invariably transported to Halesworth for these treats in farm wagons kindly lent for the occasion.

In 1923 there was a communal effort to clean and renovate the chapel. The old brick was replaced with a boarded floor; a new and more imposing pulpit was erected; benches were installed in place of the old uncomfortable forms; the lower part of the walls were panelled and the remainder distempered. A new American organ was purchased and new oil lamps were obtained. Moreover, the exterior of the chapel was repaired and painted. The work was carried out by Mr A Woodyard at a total cost of £195.

Miss H Bird, in 1935, had completed fifty years of faithful service as caretaker, this in addition to walking to the Sunday morning services in Halesworth and caring for her invalid father, Mr T Bird (who for ten years had been bedridden).

District Nurse Hilling was the organist for several years, as was Ernie Woolnough when he was only eleven or twelve. Ernie would cycle from Cookley every Sunday to play the organ when the Reverend W H Sparey was minister.

During the summer of 1950 the Reverend Peter Clarke ran a month's 'mission' in the vacation, aimed mainly at children and youth. The programme was set out thus:

On Sundays at 3pm - People's Service

On Tuesdays at 7pm - Tennis

On Wednesdays at 7.15pm - Hallo There

(a sort of Community evening with films and suchlike)

On Fridays at 7.45pm - Old Time Dancing

The whole event was quite successful.

Unfortunately, over the years the numbers in the congregation slowly dwindled. By 1970 the building was no longer in use as a chapel. In 1976, there was a grand exhibition of photographs and chapel memorabilia and in 1980 the chapel was up for sale. It was bought for £4000 and turned into a home by Alfie Lucas. Matthew Wetmore can remember working out the plans for altering the chapel on a napkin in a café in London.

Dr Richard Kell and his wife Barbara bought the place in 1986 and completed the alterations. They came with two children, Jonathan and Megan. Their third child, Emily, was actually born in the chapel. They left in 1988, moving to Linstead, and sold to Jean and Leslie Brinton. Jean is very active in the church, being, among many other commitments, a churchwarden. Until recently, she was the Wissett correspondent for the *Team Times* magazine, a position she fulfilled for several years. Leslie is a retired dentist, and now runs his wine business, 'In the Pink,' in which he excels at giving apt advice on both wine-buying and wine-tasting. His wine column in the *Team Times* makes for most enjoyable reading for Wissett connoisseurs and non-connoisseurs alike. Jean and Leslie are both keen gardeners and have turned the front of the chapel into a charming courtyard garden.

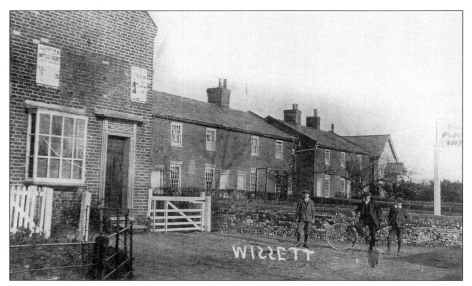

*Vista from The Plough eastwards via the cottages (Nos 2-7 The Street) to the chapel, in the early 1900s.*

## The Cottages, Nos 2 to 7 The Street

Many people in the village remember at least one of their relations living here. In the twentieth century, the families most closely connected with one or other of the cottages were the Littlewoods, the Moores, the Hunts and the Fosters.

In 1927 Emily and James Littlewood retired from Brook Hall Farm to No 5 (The Homestead), and the other cottages: Nos 2, 3, 4, 6 and 7 were rented out. Before the Littlewoods' time, No 5 had been two cottages: the end part by the path had been the home of a Mrs Jackson, who served as a midwife before the days of a district nurse. The other half of No 5, Mrs Dorothy Boast (now aged ninety-five) remembers, was where she and all her siblings were born: the eldest was Lorna, followed by Ethelbert, Alice, Gertie, Dorothy (herself the fifthborn), Florrie, Margaret, Willie, and Hazel. Gertie and Hazel Aldous both became teachers at Wissett school.

Cottage No 2 was home to Cornelius ('Nellus' ) Hunt, his brother George, and George's wife Ellen. The portly Nellus tied his corduroys with bits of 'Phyllis' (string ) under the knee, and sang loudly in church at Harvest Festival 'We Plough the Fields and Scatter' with such verve that the children were mesmerized by his lingering 'Amen.' Nellus died in 1938, aged seventy. There is a note in Wissett School Register that Nellus left school on 8 January 1880. Since the Board School had only started in 1879, Nellus had managed to evade going to school almost entirely! Ellen Hunt, or Nellie, - a rival to Nellus in portliness - once spotted a bucket of snails outside the box hedge of Sunnyside, where Elizabeth Davey was removing the creatures. 'Oh you nasty, datty little varmin, pullin' those old hodmadods about!' she cried.

Cottage No 3 was occupied by George Hunting (Poodle Cutts' nephew), his wife Elsie and daughter Vera (who married Harold Leggett, now of 14 Brickhill Bungalows).

In No 4 lived Willie and Arthur Moore (uncles of Mrs Hazel Hunt) and their mother Laura. No 6 was rented to another brother of Nellus and George: Mr Robert Hunt, with his wife Lizzie, who never had a hair out of place, and their daughter Alice. Strange and dark stories grew up around poor Alice, who, it is said, was turned into a permanent invalid by her mother, and did not leave her bedroom for thirty years from her teenage days until the day her mother died; she then got up on her crutches and walked.

Mrs Kemp lived at No 7 for a while, after she had retired from running the little post office at Blue Haw Cottage. Then Mr and Mrs Foster and Doreen, their daughter, moved here from Rose Cottage up Lodge Lane. Doreen can remember that her parents slept in the small front bedroom, while she had the tiny back one. After Doreen had married Mr Harold ('Pinto') Reeder and moved to No 15 The Street, her son Ray used to sleep up at No 7 with his grandfather Foster. Ray's father, Pinto, used to plough with horses in the fields behind.

Emily Littlewood lived on at No 5 for several years after James had died in 1933. She eventually moved to live with her daughter and son-in-law (Maggie and Arthur Pinkney) in Walpole, where she died in 1953. Both James and Emily are buried in Wissett churchyard near the little bridge over the Beck. James' funeral was the talk of the village, for he was a big man, and two of the coffin-bearers dropped their cords as they were lowering the coffin into the grave. So for two hours or longer the coffin was lodged almost vertically in the grave before it could be eased down.

Hazel Hunt's father, Mr Herbert Moore, bought the bigger block of cottages, Nos 5,

6 and 7. Herbert had previously lived at No 14 The Street. After their brother William's death, Arthur Moore moved to No 7 The Street, and Hazel with her family moved into No 5. Tragically, Hazel's brother Robert got drowned in a 'mardle' (swamp) in Malaysia in 1953 while rescuing another soldier. Robert is commemorated on a plaque in the church.

The other cottages, Nos 2, 3 and 4, were inherited by Emily Littlewood's family. The terrace was on the market for several years. The owners, the Pinkney and Littlewood brothers-in-law, wanted £350 for the cottages. They hung fire. By 1957, Mr Billy Thompson considered buying them so that his parents could live in the end one (now No 2), but: 'I'm not going over £300,' he vowed. After some to-ing and fro-ing between the cottages and the local telephone box, where considerable bargaining was done in the space of an hour, Billy and the brothers-in-law compromised at £290. Billy worked hard to modernize the end cottage ready for his parents. By 1972, both were dead, and Billy sold No 2 for £5000, while Nos 3 and 4 were sold via Flicks later. The current owners are: No 2, Fred and Pat Dick; No 3, Sheila and Brian Smith; No 4, Sharon Keating and Aidan Lunn; No 5, Hazel and her son David Hunt; No 6, Ms Rachel Thomas; and No 7, Rachel Ritchie, until recently one of the two Junior Sisters at the Patrick Stead Hospital, Halesworth, and her husband David, both computer-tutor and do-it-yourself buff, the son of Mrs Daphne Ritchie at Mill Cottage.

*Emily Littlewood*

*William Kemp in sidecar on day out at seaside, with son-in-law Sidney Johnson*

## The Plough, No 8 The Street

When John Phillips owned this property in the 1830s it was classified as a brewhouse.

Unlike The Swan Inn, it was not licensed to sell spirits in those days. According to the 1844 White's Directory, a William Howlett was landlord then, followed by William Woods. By 1858 the premises were being run by James Kemp. The Kemp family appear to have managed the brewhouse for many years, for Mrs Sarah Kemp succeeded James in the late 1860s and was still there in 1891, when, on the instructions of the beneficiaries of John Phillips' will, The Plough Inn was put up for auction. It is conjectured that Adnams the brewers bought it then. Sarah Kemp was retained as landlady, paying an annual rent of £12. Finally by 1900, Sarah had handed over the running of The Plough to William (Billy) Kemp. Billy and his wife Mary lived in Wissett for several years after leaving The Plough and Billy was a keen bellringer. He was presented with a clock in November 1931 by the parishioners of Wissett 'in appreciation of his loyal service as Church Verger for 33 years.' His and Mary's son Arthur and nephew Leonard were both killed in World War 1.

In 1906 Joseph Read was landlord until 1913 and then William Smith, who was there right through the war years until 1921. The old photographs of The Plough show 'William Smith' sign-painted over the main door. A number of retailers worked on the premises during the 1920s, including William J Spencer (1922-25), John Tripp (1926-29), and a Mr Payne from 1929-30. His daughters earned the reputation of soaking quite unspeakable objects in buckets under the communal pump in The Plough yard. People remember with fondness the days that Harry Perry ran The Plough, from 1931 right through till the end of the Second World War. With Harry's arrival, the establishment acquired 'public house' status, and spirits could be served on the premises. There used to be a hall alongside the building, adjoining the wall of No 7 cottage. Great spreads and football team dinners happened in here. On many a jolly occasion Bob Kent would sing popular songs such as 'The old kitchen kettle keeps singing a song.'

The next person to run The Plough was Mrs Ivy Spall, who moved in from the adjacent No 9 The Street with her brother Freddie Johnson in 1945. Ivy was there until 1952. Thereafter, various landlords did their best to manage the business, still under Adnams: J Gardiner (1953-55), Billie Woolnough and his wife Madge (1956-61), Mary and Wilton Blower in the 1960s, then RG Pearce followed by KC Hayes in the 1970s, and Mary and David Rayner, who arrived in 1978. In 1979, Adnams decided to sell The Plough and it was bought by Bob and Linda Wilson for some £850.

By 1977, it had become the 'biker' pub for the teenage lads. They would race up and down the village street, naked except for Doc Martin boots and tattoos. One night someone reported them to the police, and one of the boys was caught drunk in the well-lit telephone kiosk outside the old post office. He was apprehended! Another night, the boys were zooming up over Mill Road, and, looking down to the village street, they spotted by the gas station a police car flashing its blue lights. The car then sped ahead to the Halesworth end of Mill Road to cut the lads off, but they whizzed back the way they had come and were innocently sitting in The Plough when the police arrived.

The Plough saw numerous owners over the next few years. Best remembered are: 'Ray and Mo, Jack and Colin Walker, Ray and Lowry, John Plumpton and Jane and André.'

The Plough has been run for four years now by Trevor Piggott, a Sheringham man. Trevor has worked ceaselessly to create a welcoming and lively atmosphere: there are bowls nights and darts, karaoke and 'race' nights, carol-singing at Christmas and high jinks at midsummer. The Plough is a life-line for pensioners and families alike, and since the closure of the shops, is the hub of Wissett social activities.

*William Kemp in his garden at The Plough, c1900*

*William Lincolne, trustee of the chapel, and benefactor*

## No 9 and No 10 The Street

These were originally three cottages, adjoining The Plough. Anthony Barber had owned them in the 1820s, and John Phillips in the 1830s, when the tenants are named baldly as 'Howell, Balls and Hunt.' By the time of the 1891 auction they were two, and not three dwellings, tenanted by James Cooper and Robert Hunt. The buyer was Frederick Woodyard, builder of Halesworth, who paid £95, plus a little extra per annum to 'take water from the pump and well standing on the adjoining premises known as The Plough Inn.' Frederick's wife predeceased him in 1912, so when he died in 1913, his sons inherited the cottages. However, the elder son, having emigrated to Victoria, British Colombia, disclaimed his inheritance, which thus fell to Albert, the second son. In 1914 Albert, with Robert Ebenezer Haward as trustee and Nellie Pells of Beccles as mortgagee, sold to Henry Halifax, publican of Halesworth. Mr Halifax had a son at Chediston, who married Elsie Jordan of Box Farm. The tenants at No 9 and No 10 were now Robert Cooper and Henry Pearce.

In 1924, Mr Halifax, by now retired, sold to Thomas Stebbings, the farmer who lived in St Peter's Farmhouse. Halifax had bought the cottages for £62 10s, but could only sell them for £50. The tenants were named only as 'Widow Cooper and R Hammond.' Mrs Hammond, as Robert's wife, is not given a mention!

By June 1926, Robert Hammond is the only named tenant, the other cottage being vacant, and Stebbings made a big profit by selling to William Henry Boast for £150. Mr Boast settled his wife and children into the cottage next door to Mr and Mrs Hammond. Mr Johnny Nunn (formerly of Hill Farm) remembers that chickens used to sit in the windows. William Boast sold the cottages at a huge loss in July 1928, for only £55. The sole named tenant was still Robert Hammond.

The new buyer was Samuel Walls Wilson, 'gentleman, of Old Woodhouse, Upper Holton.' By the time he came to sell, four years later, he was at Winstead Magna, Huntingfield. For £45, he sold to Mrs Ivy Spall, wife of Arthur Spall and sister to the Johnson brothers: Billy, Henry, Sid, Alfie and Freddie.

This was 1934, the year of major change. There were no tenants left in the cottages, which were now derelict. Children used to pick gooseberries from the overgrown gardens. The Johnsons knocked the cottages down, and built the two semi-detached houses, Nos 9 and 10, that are what we see today. Ivy managed to raise a mortgage 'on land and cottages' in June 1935, after the new houses were built, and repaid the mortgage in August 1945. She sold the pair of houses in October 1945 to Charles Richard Sugden Richardson, 'Civil Engineer' of Wissett for £2000, Ashley Green, 'Master Blacksmith at The Forge' being a witness to the conveyance.

Alfie Johnson and his wife Mildred occupied No 10, while No 9 was empty. For the first time, in 1945, the building was re-classified as Jubilee House, No 10 The Street, and Sunnyside, No 9. Mr Richardson, farmer at The Pines, invited Percy and Elizabeth Davey and their little daughter, Gloria, newly returned to Wissett by removal lorry, straight into Sunnyside to live, instead of the tiny cottage at the bottom of The Pines drive where they were expecting to be housed. Alfie and Percy were both employees of Richardson.

Gloria, who became a pupil at Wissett school, was a wonderful young pianist, and her harmonies would float through the walls to the joy of Mildred Holden next door. Mrs Davey chuckles as she remembers Scorcher West, the chimney sweep, who every few months had to come and clear No 9's chimneys. These had been designed so narrow at the top that they trapped the 'sutt.'

'Cor, gal! ya go' a lo' o' ol' hard sutt up here! Ya been barnin' a lo' o' wood, gal!' he would exclaim as he spat into the soot.

By 1949 or 50, Philip Clarke had come and 'wired up' the houses on behalf of Mr Richardson, with an early form of electric circuitry. On April 10 1956, Charles Richardson conveyed Sunnyside to Manor Farm (Wissett) Limited, which he ran as a business. In 1960, Alfie Johnson, who had served in the Eighth Army in the war, and was

*The Plough and thatched cottages, Nos 9 and 10, with their horizontal garden fences, in about 1895*

*The same vista, in about 1970.*

Mr Richardson's foreman, was found dead one day near his workplace. Between then and 1964, his widow Mildred married PC William Holden who had sold Bond's Farm a week before Alfie's death. In 1964, Richardson sold Jubilee House to Mildred, now Mrs Holden, for £1650.

In 1966, Richardson died and the Holdens moved into Sunnyside. They sold Jubilee House for £1950 to Mr and Mrs Lyon of Wissett Stores, the shop opposite. This is the first conveyance that mentions electricity (a shared cable between No 9 and No 10), and a public sewer in the street, with an inspection cover on No 9 premises to serve both houses. Permission was still needed to extract water from the pump and well on The Plough precincts.

John and Margaret Lyon remained at the shop while getting an Improvement Grant of £145 in February 1968. They sold Jubilee House in 1969 for £2800 to Louis Botha Marsh of Brentwood in Essex. Mr and Mrs Marsh's daughter, Mrs Margaret Oddy, had come to live in Sunnyside with her husband, David, and their sons, Robert, Stephen and Philip. The Oddys were managing the shop opposite for Ivy Spall.

In 1978, the widowed Florence Marsh sold to Mr and Mrs Gardiner from Hardwicke in Gloucestershire. Their buying price was £13,000 and the conveyance was witnessed by DC Rayner, landlord of The Plough. Terence Lincoln Gardiner and his wife Margaret lived in Jubilee House for eight years, before selling in 1986 to the Weavers who came from Walpole. This time the house fetched £25,500. Jenny Weaver, a schoolteacher, died tragically young in 1997, and her widower, Roger, moved out reluctantly and put the house on the market. Eventually in the spring of 1999, Kim and Tom Croysdill moved in from Holton with young Jenna, Donovan and Maxwell. Kim remembers staying as a girl in Forge House with the Talbots, and witnessing some dangerous escapades. Micheline, one of the Talbot daughters, fell out of the back bedroom window once, and broke her leg.

The present owners of Sunnyside are the teachers Christine and Finlay Martin, who live with their son Alexander and assorted animals.

## No 12 The Street

This house, built by Paul Maulden after his parents had moved to Halesworth in the 1970s, is on the site of the 'double tenement' that was sold off by auction in 1891 under the direction of John Phillips' beneficiaries, the three Button sisters. At that time, the two tenants were 'Barber' and 'Chipperfield'- no first names and no other family members are given! The cottages were bought by Harriet Dunnett. Her will of 16 October 1894 bequeathed all her estate to her daughter Florence Elizabeth Dunnett. The cottages remained in Florence's ownership until they were sold in 1932.

From the early 1920s, people can vividly remember the Birds, the Millers and the Todds, who inhabited these two cottages. Hannah Bird, (born circa 1859), who lived in the left-hand one, was granddaughter of a Methodist minister and nursemaid to her invalid father. In the right-hand cottage were Walter Miller, his son Herbert ('Spider'), and his daughter Mrs Ethel Todd, a dressmaker whose husband George had been in the navy, caught TB and died at only twenty-nine in 1926. Walter Miller worked over the road as a blacksmith for the Green brothers at the forge, and Spider was a fisherman off the coast near Lowestoft. After a voyage, he would supply the whole village with herring and plaice that Ted Cutts would prepare in his smokehouse by Saffron Cottage. Spider would also shower sweets on the local children. His brother, Bob, used to cycle from Rumburgh to help Walter. Apparently, Ethel and her brothers were all profoundly deaf, and being devout chapel-goers, would sing joyfully and loudly, oblivious to the decibels issuing from their lips. Ethel was the first to accept a deaf-aid; the others were suspicious of such a gadget.

Hannah Bird, whilst being a devoted daughter and ardent chapel Sunday School teacher in Wissett, had her moments of fun too. She used to take in washing from The

*View down Wissett Street in the 1970s*

Red House at the same time as a suave butler nicknamed Little Bill worked there. The jokes about what she found in the pockets of Little Bill's trousers were circulated quietly round The Swan Inn. Hannah lived until 1941, and was succeeded by Cyril and Lily Maulden, parents of Jacqueline and Paul.

Cyril was a marvellous gardener, and the front of his cottage used to be ablaze with flowers, by all accounts. Lily became great friends with Freda Kerrison, who was new to the village about the same time, and the two have remained friends for almost sixty years. It was wartime when they first met, and Lily, who cycled daily to Beccles hospital where she worked, was stopped as if she were an enemy spy almost every day by the wartime checkout guards on the Bungay Road.

Ethel Todd lived next door to the Mauldens until her death in 1966. It was shortly afterwards that Lily and Cyril began to think about moving. Their son Paul, who runs his own heating, engineering and plumbing business, put into practice his plans for a completely new house. This is the one that is here now. Paul and his wife Elizabeth have lived in it until just recently.

The new owners, who moved from Rumburgh, are Graham and Carol Steele. Their two grown up children are Nicola and Christopher. Both Graham and Christopher work for Ernest Doe & Sons.

## Nos 13,14,15,16, and 17 The Street

These cottages figure in the 'abstract of title,' after the death of their owner John Phillips in 1846, as 'situate and being in Wissett aforesaid then in the occupon (occupation) of Hammond Rackham Shipley Baker and Bird.' One can only surmise that these five names represent families whose graves line the church path leading from the bridge.

Along with the other 'lots' leading to The Plough, this row of five, with 1¼ acres of 'outbuildings yards gardens and premises' was auctioned off in 1891. The buyer was Harriet Dunnett, who also bought the 'double tenement' next door to the east. Harriet's daughter, Florence Elizabeth, inherited all seven cottages. Her estate was put up for auction in 1932. By this time, the inhabitants of these 'five several tenements' were: Walter Kerrison at No 13; RJ Read at No 14; Mr and Mrs Cobb at No 15; Mrs Sally Foster at No 16; and Charles (Charlie) Kerrison, Walter's brother, at No 17. Mr Charles Kerrison senior had lived at No 17, and thought nothing of riding on his tricycle to Peasenhall regularly. Together with Walter, Charles had been a dedicated bell-ringer (his prowess is recorded under the heading 'The Church Bells'). Another son, George, had married Lizzie Aldous from Pear Tree Farm. Walter's wife, Nellie Mina, had died distressingly young in 1916, leaving a little boy, Bob, to be brought up by Walter and his sister Amy. It was Walter who bought the five cottages. He had stayed in Wissett after service in the Royal Essex Regiment in World War I.

Like most of their neighbours, the Kerrisons kept pigs, fed on protein-rich lucerne grown in allotment strips behind the cottages. Bob and Walter worked as gardeners and looked after Rover, Miss Login's huge dog at Wissett Grange.

The next excitement in their lives was the arrival from Norfolk of the sprightly young Freda Wild. She had come to work in Spexhall at Steward and Patteson, the brewers, and

*Members of the Kerrison family -*
*Charles and his wife Mary,*
*Samuel and George.*

then as lady's maid to Lady Alcock of Ilketshall Hall. Freda recalls serving tea to Yehudi Menuhin, Lady Alcock's nephew, and accompanying Lady Alcock in her Rolls Royce on numerous trips to Cheltenham Races.

Freda married Bob Kerrison early in the Second World War years and came to live at No 17. Times were hard; Bob was away in the navy and Freda worked in the munitions factory in Leiston. She cycled to Leiston very early on Mondays, lodged there during the week, and cycled back at weekends. She even had the energy to play women's football regularly, and was in her factory team that played against the WRENS and the land army girls.

Later, Freda bought a Lambretta scooter on which she often motored up to Norwich to visit her mother. It was quite common to be under the flight path of German bombers. Whilst Freda and her neighbour Gladys Codling (by then at No 16) were blackberrying by Wissett Lodge one day, a warplane swooped so low that they could easily see the swastika. Another job Freda undertook for two years or so was as post-lady for Mrs Salmon at No 18. Freda's 'beat' was up Rumburgh Street and round all the Gray's Lane farms. Once a month, a man known as a 'timer' cycled with Freda, to keep check on how long it took her to do the circuit.

*Eric Stollery with a friend in 1951, during the time of the Korean War.*

As well as at No 16, where Gladys Codling and her husband Ernie (a horseman) lived during the war, there had been a number of changes of tenant in the other cottages. The Cobbs had left No 15, and Pinto Reeder was there with his wife Doreen and their children Barbara and Ray. At No 14, Herbert Moore had been living for a while, followed by Billy Wilby and family. When Billy died in 1945, aged sixty-six, there was a big funeral for him in the church. He had been headman for Lord Stradbroke and for Mrs Alice Richardson for a total of thirty-six years. He left a widow, two daughters, five grandchildren and two great-grandchildren.

After Walter died, Freda devoted herself to looking after anyone who needed her loving care. This included her husband Bob and young Clive Stollery, who had become a neighbour at No 15 with his father Eric.

Although Freda no longer plays football, she has perfected the art of playing bowls, and her sideboard is a shining display of trophies and cups that she and Eric have won between them. Eric has restored a number of the old properties in Wissett, including parts of The Swan, with skilled brickwork and Suffolk-style 'lump' plastering. He learnt the trade, he says, from one of the master-builders of Aldeburgh, a Mr Read.

The present owners of No 14 are the Starkey family, who use the cottage in the holidays. No 13 is up for sale, since the owners, John Davies and family, now back from the Far East, have bought a bigger house in Linstead.

*NB. Since going to press, Freda Kerrison, much-loved friend and neighbour, has died March 2001.*

*WI Fancy Dress party, 1930s. The ladies, in gypsy costume are, from left to right: Nurse Christine Hilling, Mrs Salmon, Mrs Godbold, Mrs Todd, Ethel Cutts, Mrs Aldred.*

## The Old Post Office, No 18 The Street

This Georgian cottage has records dating from 1812, when it was owned by Anthony Barber. By 1829, the premises were jointly owned by Barber and the Reverend Richard Crutwell of Spexhall, who came to a sad end, being thrown out of his carriage by his runaway horse after a cart-crash near Fleet Street, London, in 1846.

It is likely that there was an older cottage on the site, which Barber and the clerical financier developed. At all events, the place was held in trust for Mary Algar, and stayed within the Algar family until the 1880s. The Algars were traditionally tailors and schoolteachers. Then the Greens took over, blacksmiths and farmers, to whom John and George Green at the forge were related. The property was put up for auction on 4 October 1899, and Frederick Charles Fenn was the highest bidder at £125. He turned the cottage into two tenements for 'Bousland' and 'Salter'. It is unclear when exactly the cottage became the village post office but it was probably during the time of Mrs Sarah and Mr Richard Salmon, who owned the cottage from 1905. The next transfer was to Richard's daughter-in-law, Florence Elizabeth (Fanny) Salmon of Bramfield, in 1931. When she was down the back garden tending her vegetables, Fanny would hear Charlie Kerrison's voice trolling from the privy next door:

> 'There is a happy land, far, far away
> Where little piggies rain three times a day
> Oh! you should see them run
> When they see the butcher come
> Three slices off their bums
> Three times a day!'

Not even the stately Mrs Salmon escaped the fate that befell so many villagers: death by drowning. It happened a long time after she had left Wissett. But Mrs Salmon's death was rather horrible, as the Reverend Ben Angell of Walpole chapel related quite recently. It was he who found her body frozen in The Folly by the quayside in Halesworth.

After Fanny Salmon had retired from the post office, Audrey and Stanley Spinks arrived in the 1950s, with Shirley their daughter, and Harry Rice, Audrey's father. Harry was ninety-three in 1971, the oldest resident in Wissett. Many people can remember Mrs Spinks in the 'shop' part of the cottage, handing out sweets to them when they were children. In 1978, the Witheys took over, followed by Mr Frederick Gregory, the last person to run the shop in 1983. The present owner, Diana Fernando, moved into the village to be near her mother and other relatives. She works as a volunteer with New Thresholds, the Beccles-based charity that helps people suffering with mental illness and other health problems return to employment.

## Cobbler's Cottage, No 19 The Street

The Reverend Derek Tilston lives with his wife Dorothy in this pretty cottage. The Hawood dynasty of non-conformist benefactors owned it for much of the nineteenth century. There are records from 1894 of Frederick Haward there as shopkeeper and shoemaker. By the left-hand wall of the front garden, bordering the road, was a little barnlike dwelling where the cobbler mended the villagers' shoes and farm boots. The last resident cobbler was called Waxy Hard by the boys of Dick Foster's generation - his real name being, in true family tradition, Freddie Haward. He had a pony and trap, and on the left side of the cottage as you face it, there was a door through to the cobbler's workshop. In the front window, bordering the street, were rows of tins of shoe-polish and saddle soap and hob-nailed boots for the farmworkers. The village pranksters of Jimmy Cutts' boyhood years would clamber up onto the cobbler's shed roof and stuff the chimneys with sacks so that the smoke would belch out in all directions.

'Bast the jolly Dickens!' Waxy would exclaim.

After Waxy's time, a Mrs Murphy moved in, between 1929 and 1930, with her little son known as Boyan. Mrs Murphy had bright red hair and a 'husband' who came some weekends. The schoolmistress Miss Howell lodged with her.

The next residents, from about 1931, were Mrs Isabella (Bella) Rumsby and her brother George ('Friday') Davy. Elizabeth Taylor remembers that, as a girl in a short dress and long thin legs, she was nicknamed 'Legs' by Bella. When Elizabeth was about fourteen, and starting to dress up with crimping slides in her hair, Bella would exclaim, 'I see Legs has got her aeroplanes on - is she going out tonight?'

For forty years, Friday had been courting a woman who was live-in cook at Bungay St Mary School. When Bella died in about 1935, Friday married his sweetheart, Sarah, only to die himself a year on. Mrs Sarah Davy is still pictured by many, biking up to her sister Lizzie at Spexhall, and coming back laden with driftwood precariously balanced all over the handlebars and pillion. Sarah was often seen scurrying along Wissett Street bearing a long-handled black saucepan of steaming food for Nessie Whatling, who was growing poorly, at No 25.

Mrs Dorothy Tilston remembers that, before her own family, a Mrs Mary Stocker lived here with her two beautiful daughters, Bryony and Portia. Apparently one of them fell terribly in love with a Talbot boy at Forge House. Together they planted a chestnut tree as a lovers' tryst in the back garden of Cobbler's Cottage, but it had quite outgrown the space allowed for it when the Tilstons moved here, and had to be felled.

Dorothy and Derek are gifted teachers and artists, Derek a painter and Dorothy chiefly a potter. Although they retired from the ministry when they came to Wissett in the early 1990s, Derek assists in the Team's services when needed. They greatly enjoy entertaining their grandchildren in the garden studio.

*Waxy Hard the cobbler's workshop, in front of No 19 The Street.*

## St Peter's Farm Bungalow

The original cottage on this site was part of the farmstead of St Peter's owned in the 1830s and 40s by John Crabtree, Lord of Halesworth Manor. It was at that time run by John Phillips. Mrs Dora Warren recalls how her grandfather, Mr Frederick Oxborough, whose forefathers had emigrated from Ireland, moved into this cottage with his wife Nellie ('Nana') when it belonged to Wissett Hall. They had a black Dexter cow. Their daughter Anna Maria (Annie) later married George ('Pod') Taylor, and went to live at Saffron Cottage. The other children were: Bertie, who died in infancy; Charlie, who settled in Long Melford; Eliza, who moved away; and William, known as Uncle Winter because of his striking resemblance to his mother's forbears, who were Winters. Little Bertie had a special book, and after he had died Nellie used to say to her granddaughters, 'If you're good, I'll let you look at Bertie's book.' The favourite poem in this book of rhymes had the disconcerting title of *In Search of Pork*.

Freddie and Nellie Oxborough were legendary. Freddie used to pump the bellows of the church organ during the singing of the Sunday hymns. Years afterwards his granddaughter, Dora Warren, who had to sit in for him occasionally, found 'F.OX' carved onto the side of the organ in the wood. Dora knew it was her Gran'dad getting bored. Annie's daughters used to accompany Nellie on hot summer days up to the meadows and woodland behind their cottage. Nellie would exercise their pet rabbits, allowing them to graze while Dora, Margie and Elizabeth made daisy-chains among the buttercups. Nellie would fill her 'mentle' (apron) with sticks for kindling from the ash trees.

*Nellie Oxborough at her garden gate*

53

*Dora Taylor, Nellie and Freddie Oxborough's granddaughter, outside St Peter's Farm*

Nellie and Fred had a linnet in a cage for fifteen years in the dark little kitchen on the side of the house next to Cobbler's Cottage. Sometimes they would put the cage in the front room to 'sun' it. The bird seemed cheerful enough, singing often. Annie was a game young lady, who used to play Irish jigs by ear on the violin and accordion at functions in The Swan Inn. As a young woman, she went into service at Wissett Lodge, and once her children were grown up, became a post-mistress. To do the rounds, Annie bought an Austin Ruby car. It was in World War II, but Annie taught herself to drive on the meadow that was behind their cottage. 'Hop! Hop! Hop!' she'd say as the little Ruby stalled and smoke poured out of the exhaust. Notwithstanding, she'd jerk her way around the countryside.

Younger relatives talk of Nellie's kindness. She was often called to act as midwife, along with Mrs Jackson, in the years before Nurse Hilling, and she was always surrounded by children. Cyril Maulden was part of the family fold from the age of four, and many events stand out in his memory. One such was his sighting of the Pulham Pig airship, the R33, floating over Wissett in 1925. Not only can Cyril describe the torn nose of the damaged Pig that was adrift from its mooring at Pulham airfield, but a tiny, buzzing, yellow plane, possibly a de Havilland 'Hummingbird,' that was trying to latch onto the Pig in a rescue attempt. It was a Sunday, and half the villagers were out walking in their Sunday best. Cyril was up Gray's Lane. Long afterwards, men in The Plough remembered how in those hard times unemployed boys would rush to Pulham whenever volunteers were needed to 'trail the ropes' as an airship was eased down to the ground after breaking loose from its mooring mast. They'd get two shillings (10p) or half a crown (12$\frac{1}{2}$ p) for their quite dangerous work: hanging on to trailing ropes below the Pig meant being tossed up and down over hedgerows and walls, and frequently limbs were broken.

Another momentous occasion was the earth tremor that vibrated through Wissett in June 1931. It was just before midnight between a Saturday and a Sunday, when most people were in bed. Nellie Oxborough's younger relatives take up the tale: 'There was a roar like a lorry, then all this shaking. Everyone had their heads out of their windows upstairs. Ewers rattled on washstands. Next day on the wireless it said that the earth was re-balancing itself. It was felt all over Suffolk.' Nellie herself could cast her mind back to another quake, fifty years or so previously, when 'all the china fell off the whatnot.' This was the Colchester earthquake of 1884.

The most dire quake in the village was, however, when the landmine was dropped in 1943. Nellie was actually dead and lying in her coffin in the parlour with the shutters closed. The long clock (that Pod Taylor had brought back from Holland) stopped, and the shutters burst open. One of Nellie's granddaughters, Margie, rushed to guard the coffin and could not be found for ages by her worried mother.

By 1945, the cottage was occupied by a Mrs Gertie Daws (née Thurlow, sister to Ethel Cutts). After she had gone, the buildings were in rather a sorry state. Mr Hector Calver bought the premises and land for a small sum. Hector's son, Ray, and his wife Angie live in the bungalow they built on the site. Ray was born in The Old Vicarage in Wissett and worked for British Telecom. After he married Angie, who came from Southwold, his job took the pair to Lowestoft and Coventry. There are three children:

Chris, Paul and Karen. The family came back to Wissett and built the bungalow in 1980. Ray has been organizing the Horticulture Show for several years and is a member of the Bowls Club. He is also a parish councillor.

*Ray Calver in 1958, aged about fifteen*

## St Peter's Farmhouse, No 20 The Street

In the early years of the nineteenth century, John Crabtree, one of the big family of solicitors connected with the Crosses ( of the present-day firm of Cross, Ram & Co in Halesworth ) owned the land here and the neighbouring site, which is now Ray Calver's.

Tom Stebbings the horse-dealer lived here in the 1920s. He was, remembers Billy Thompson, a big man who had a horse and cart that just held him. He'd wear a check shirt and bright yellow waistcoat and a watch-chain - a 'flamboyant character,' according to Miss Lizzie Eagle Bott. Tom's precious son, Russell, died of diphtheria when he was only about four, and Annie Taylor took her young daughters over to see the dead boy, as it was the custom for everyone to pay their last respects. One little daughter, Elizabeth, had bad dreams as a consequence, and Mrs Stebbings, Russell's mother, tried to comfort her with the present of a small wooden toy coffin, whose lid slid back to reveal a naked, white, china doll with ramrod stiff legs. This upset Elizabeth even more, so her mother secretly buried the miniature coffin and its contents in her garden at Saffron Cottage. To this day, nobody knows exactly where the gruesome offering lies.

After Tom, the property, together with the other St Peter's property next to it, was bought by the Scrimgeours of Wissett Hall. The Scrimgeours installed a much-needed district nurse, Christina Zipporah (after Moses' wife) Hilling, who is mentioned in various directories from 1929 to 1945. She is remembered with fondness by Mrs Joyce Thompson and by Mrs Doreen Reeder as the midwife who 'did' all the village births. She had her parents and brother living with her; and Miss Ballard, the schoolteacher, boarded here before moving to the bungalow next to Arthur Frost. Christina used to give 'great

*The Lockwoods' bungalow being renovated.*

56

parties' with delicious teas and poetry readings.

Afterwards, the farmhouse was put up for public auction and Mr Leonard (Lenny) Reeder and his wife Harriet bought it. They had moved from Hill House Farm up near Rumburgh on Leonard's retirement. When Harriet died in 1963, their son John, with his wife Mary and daughter Angela, moved in with Leonard to care for him. Their second daughter Sally was born here. Leonard died in 1979 and John and Mary stayed on for a further two years, until 1981, when the house was sold to Clive and Pat Chambers and their young daughters: Kay, then nine, and Penny, three. Mary and John Reeder moved to Chediston for a few years.

Mr Jeremy Sindall lives at St Peter's Farmhouse now with his mother and sisters, Lucy and Susan. Jeremy breeds doves and runs a removal business, while Susan teaches at Henstead School and the others grow and sell flowers and plants.

## Three Bungalows (Nos 21, 22 and 23 )

In the early 1800s this plot was an orchard owned by John Oldring, the publican at The Swan. A century later, it was known as Half Acre and owned by Mrs Sutherland, who lived in part of No 25 The Street. There are villagers today who remember Half Acre as a field of maize, where the boys used to make pathways between the high stalks.

As part of the war effort, the field was built on and developed by Arthur Frost of Corner Farm. Arthur built his own bungalow on the third of the plot nearest The Swan, and retired here. He then built the middle bungalow, No 22,  for Miss Marjorie Ballard. She was head teacher at Rumburgh school until its closure in the late 1950s. She went on to a school in Halesworth. When Arthur's wife, Rosetta, died, and Arthur was becoming increasingly blind, Miss Ballard cooked for him daily. She arranged the food on the plate for him like a clock: 'Peas at the top, that's 12 o'clock; 'taters at the bottom, that's 6 o'clock,' she'd say, so that Arthur could feel his way round. Poor Miss Ballard died in 1982: she went away on holiday, never to return. The present owners of 'Wayside,' No 22, John and Mary Reeder, moved back into Wissett after their time in Chediston. They have made a marvellous garden, and with their green fingers, help nearly everyone else in the village.

Arthur built the third bungalow, No 21, for Mr Bynes and his daughter, Miss Bynes, who worked for Arthur as a land army girl. Mr Percy De'Ath bought the place in the 1970s, and moved over from Saffron Cottage with his wife who could no longer manage the stairs. Although Percy is now a widower and lives on his own, he is very independent in spite of eyesight problems. He loves visitors, and is a cheerful conversationalist.

Marcia and Clive Lockwood bought the bungalow that Arthur had lived in. With their combined skills, they have completely renovated and re-clad it with brick and plaster. A carved pheasant graces the front wall. Clive is a partner in a building firm, while Marcia works for a new-age music company called New World Music which was started some fifteen years ago by Colin and Carmen Wilcox.

## The Old Swan *(formerly The Swan Inn)*

This four-hundred-year-old building was once part of a farm with a large orchard. In the seventeenth century it was licensed as a pork butcher's and then as a public house. The strip of land adjoining the orchard was very rich soil and had been used for hemp-growing. It all belonged to John Oldring by 1840, and later was bought by Lacon's of Yarmouth, the Norfolk brewers.

Many publicans ran The Swan over the years. Samuel Gooch is listed in 1844, Samuel Hollingworth in 1858, Robert Adams and his wife Caroline (née Thurlow) in 1861, James Harvey in 1864 and 69, and the Hurren brothers, James and George, from 1873-92. The next landlord was John Hancey, who ran The Swan from 1893 or 94 until the First World War. John's father, David, came from Ilketshall and married Elizabeth Mason in 1830. Their three children were all born in Wissett: Betsy in 1833, William in 1836, and John in 1837. William married Mary Ann Banthorpe of Cransford and brought her to Wissett, where all of their eight children were born: William Charles, George Emanuel, Fanny, Alvenah, Frederick, Levi, Delilah and Joseph. William and Mary Ann Hancey emigrated to Australia with some of their children, including Frederick. Ms DL Hancey of Westminster, Western Australia, is Frederick's granddaughter, and still in touch with Wissett.

Meanwhile, John Hancey who married Emma Peck in 1862 stayed in Wissett all his life, and was succeeded at The Swan by Albert Boast in 1916. Albert's son Ernest (Ernie) went to Framlingham College and grew up to become a stockbroker. He courted Dorothy Aldred (from No 5 The Street) who at that time was governess to Christina Pawlyn at The

Old Vicarage. In the late 1920s, after Albert, a Mr Hines ran the inn for a short while. Friends of his daughter June recall playing by The Swan cartsheds, which housed the old privies.

Ernest ('Puff') Seaman served at The Swan throughout the 1930s. The colourful Puff 's wife is remembered for her savoury fish and chips 'fry-ups' over her oil-stove in the annexe to the left of The Swan. She finally gave way to Lily Constance and Lily's brother Billy, who moved in.

Local people to this day still muse over the 'best publicans ever': Sid and Vera Aldridge, who managed The Swan during

*The landlords of The Swan, Sidney and Vera Aldridge, with their son, Pat, during the Second World War*

*The Swan, with the huge chestnut tree in the foreground, 1940s*

and after the war. It was a dramatic era in Wissett's history. Villagers remember the bombs exploding nearby and glass shattering. Jo Aldridge, one of Vera and Sid's sons, can recall Vera's grandmother (Nellie Oxborough ) running to the door at The Swan when the whole of the room lit up with a bomb blast: 'They're coming! they're coming!' she cried, holding the door fast shut.

American airmen based locally were frequent visitors, bringing with them plentiful supplies of sweets. So much so that the pub dog was named 'Candy' in their honour.

Certain other frequenters were legendary. In particular, Mr Rowe of Valley Farm. He was, it is told, the first one into The Swan of a morning. He used to throw back a double whiskey straight down, holding the glass with both hands. 'I'll have another,' he'd say to his shocked land-boy. Mr Rowe would then leap into his beige Austin 10 car and continue his rounds: The Plough, then the Halesworth pubs, and back through Chediston ending up at Valley Farm, 'having encompassed some sixty pubs.'

After the Aldridges, Pat and Jack Bower ran the premises until 1972, when its licence was not renewed and Lacon's considered it no longer feasible to run it as a public house. It was then bought at auction, to be used as a dwelling, by Walter Lamb, who had served in Canada during the war and lived in Italy. Having worked in the decorative business for Syrie Maugham (Somerset Maugham's accomplished wife) he had a real feel for sensitive restoration, and The Swan by then was in need of considerable overhaul. So Walter set about converting the inn back to its seventeenth-century vernacular. He had a cart which he would take to market laden with antiques, ephemera and china. He'd return with carefully-

59

chosen materials for renovating The Swan. 'He 'undid' the building,' reflects Maryanne Wilkins, the present owner. 'He took out everything. The doors and windows were continually metamorphosing.' The Gothic windows of the back kitchen were salvaged from the village hall, which was being renovated. Walter also attended to the loft, for there had been no stairwell to it in the eighteenth century, and he thatched the roof.

Maryanne remembers Walter with great fondness. She and her husband Bartholomew had been coming to The Swan for many years to buy antiques from Walter, and eventually bought The Swan in about 1980. Walter died in 1983 and was buried in Darlinton.

During the 1980s, Eric Stollery ( who lives at No 16 The Street ) did much of the pinkish plastering to repair the Suffolk 'clay lump' walls in the kitchen areas.

The brick building to the right of The Swan was where Mr Boast had reared pigeons, and the bright blue stable door still has a round hole near the bottom. This was where the pigeons flew in and out, even though it was curiously near the ground. Mrs Dorothy Boast, now aged ninety-five in this millennium year, can confirm this tale with a twinkle in her eye, although younger people might think the hole was for the cats to get in to catch the mice in the granary!

*The Old Swan today*

*Gothic Lodge*

## Gothic Lodge

This was built by Mr Walter Lamb while he owned The Swan in the 1970s. Apparently he had a wonderful eye for old doors and timber that he could match to existing styles and make appear 'antique.'

When Walter was dying, he wanted Bartholomew and Maryanne Wilkins to buy the lodge, which they did. It is currently occupied by John Gazeley, the picture-restorer and art historian.

## No 25 The Street

Matthew Wetmore, the present owner, recalls: 'The house has its origins in the fourteenth century and is one of the oldest in Wissett. It was probably the bailiff's house - the village pound was located across the Beck where the chestnut tree and bench now stand.

The dwelling was built as a hall house - that is, the western half of the property had no first floor and the evening fire would be built in the middle of the space. In the loft is the remains of the crown-post roof, still blackened from the fire smoke. In the eastern half, the family slept upstairs and would have brought their smallholding livestock into the downstairs area each night. Three chimney stacks and the rest of the first floor were added in the sixteenth century. The south facing front was covered over with bricks and sash windows added in the Victorian era. The thatch was taken off and the roof tiled over in the 1950s.'

The property was owned in the 1830s by Robert Tacon and occupied by Richard Allen. At one time the place was divided into three dwellings.

61

In the 1920s, a Mrs Debenham occupied the western end. She struggled to bring up her rather large family. Her little son Kenny had just started at Wissett school when he was run over by Mr Gorst of Valley Farm. Kenny had darted onto the road from Wissett Grange driveway straight into the oncoming car. At the funeral, all the boys from the school had to carry the coffin. Cyril Maulden was one of the schoolboys, and remembers they were all given one shilling wages as coffin bearers. But Nellie Oxborough, Cyril's adoptive mother, insisted that Cyril give his shilling to Mrs Debenham.

By 1945, Mr Frederick Woods, farm bailiff to John Lawn of Wissett Place, had retired to No 25 with his wife Ellen Alice, whose funeral is recorded in 1958. Freddie was looked after for his remaining life by Nessie Whatling, John Howlett's aunt. Mrs Sutherland, owner of Corner Farm and the orchard 'Half Acre,' lived in the middle cottage, while her daughters, Clara and Mabel, came and went.

Matthew Wetmore writes that he moved from London to Wissett in 1988, and spent two years renovating No 25. He and Cara were married in 1990, and they run the Delicatessen in Halesworth. Matthew was chairman of the Wissett Community Council for a number of years and instigated the Wissett Treacle Fair. He prepared and organized the publication of Lizzie Eagle Bott's memoirs, *I Looked Over The Gate* to coincide with that lady's ninetieth birthday.

## Lilac Manor

People can remember Corner Farm that stood here long before Lilac Manor was built.

The farm had belonged in the 1830s to the powerful landowner Robert Tacon, and had been managed then, along with Red House Farm, by Richard Allen.

By the 1920s, Corner Farm belonged to Mrs Sutherland, who lived at No 25 The Street. The farm was quite run-down, with all sorts of derelict sheds and barns.

Meanwhile, Arthur Frost, who had married Rosetta (Rosie) Calver of Bond's Farm, hired Corner Farm from Mrs Sutherland. 'He farmed after a fashion - he was new to farming,' Mr Billy Thompson now remembers. Arthur was the local milkman, hence his nickname, 'Creamy.' When Mrs Sutherland died, Rosie ('she wasn't no beauty, but she had MIND') bought Corner Farm and the Half Acre orchard to the east of The Swan which had also been Mrs Sutherland's.

Creamy was obviously a good sort, but had an eye for the girls. While Rosie contemplated the world, leaning over the half-stable door of the farmhouse, her husband was out and about. He had a 'Clino'- a grey car with a soft top and a dickey seat. 'I'll take you for a drive in the Clino tonight,' he'd tell the village girls. It was Sally Foster at No 16 The Street who used to call out to Creamy: 'I wonder they don't lead you around with a rosette on, like they do on stallions!'

Mr Syer, who had previously farmed there during World War 1, lived in a tiny cottage attached to Corner Farm.

'He had a little old horse and trap,' Mr Billy Thompson recalls. 'Of course he had a wife too.....He was a rate-collector and overseer of the parish. Mind you, the building regulations were different then.　　No planning... Always walked with his hands behind his back. A gentleman.'　　'A gentleman-penguin,' muses someone else, who was young when Mr Syer was old. Apparently he retired to Nessie Whatling's, at No 25 The Street.

After Rosie Frost had died, Creamy remained the owner of Corner Farm, although he moved to the bungalow on his Half Acre field that he had developed. In the 1960s, the farm was sold to Arthur Sterry, who had the farmhouse condemned.

The modern house, Lilac Manor, that is on the site now, was built in 1988. Although it stood empty for ten years, Jason King (of the firm MR King), his wife, Leanne, and baby son, Miles, are there now. All traces of the old shacks have been replaced by smooth lawns.

## Corner House

This house was built in the early 1960s by Arthur Sterry who had bought Corner Farm from Arthur Frost. Because the farmhouse itself had to be condemned, Mr Sterry got permission to build on the corner opposite where Corner House now stands. After Mr Sterry, the house was sold to Mona Stone whose husband Ron was head of the then secondary school in Halesworth. Anne and David Andrews bought from the Stones in the 1970s, and have lived in the house ever since. Until recently David ran his company, Andrew's Electonics, while Anne, formerly teaching at Cookley and Walpole schools, has been teaching for some ten years at Edgar Sewter School in Halesworth. The couple are active members of parish committees.

*Corner House*

## The Old Forge: *Beck Cottage, No 33 The Street;*
*Forge House, No 32; The Old Forge Cottage; and Blue Haws, No 31*

These four dwellings, plus the extra addition to the west side of No 31, constituted the forge complex of cottages, stables, forge and yards with outbuildings that was owned in the 1830s by Joseph Berry and Henry Birch, and occupied by George Hufflett, blacksmith, and John Aldridge, bricklayer/whiting manufacturer. The two main cottages, Beck Cottage and Forge House, go back to the seventeenth century at least. There are references to shopkeepers, tailors, dressmakers and smiths in Wissett harking back into the distance of time, although it is not possible to pinpoint exactly where they lived within this complex.

## Beck Cottage, No 33 The Street

This was a shop until recently. From about the time of the First World War, the earliest memory of people now in the village is of a colourful lady called Rosa Read, who wore a green tammy and had a strange way of balancing her scales. When a child asked for two ounces of sweets, if the handful of sweets tipped the scales just over, Mrs Read would remove one sweet, bite it in half, give the young customer one half and eat the other piece herself. If it was sugar you wanted, and Rosa hadn't any in stock, she'd say, 'but I have flour!' Or, ' I have some nice sugar!' when you wanted tea. Joe and Rosa Read had four sons, Percy, Roly, Arnold (Ernie) and Vic. Ernie married Phyllis, and the couple moved to Halleluia Cottage. Vic was a fisherman and married Minnie Nunn.

The shop passed in the late twenties to the management of Bob and Amelia Alice (Millie) Kent, who had four children: Robert Leslie (Lester), Margaret, Alan and Janet. Madge Cutts and Elizabeth Taylor as girls used to take Alan out in his pram. When Bob moved on to Heveningham Hall Farm Cottage, he had four more children.

By 1937, Jacqueline and Richard Shepherd were running the shop, which was open on Sundays. Dick worked the petrol pumps, but he had a hump-back so had to balance it by leaning far backwards to siphon the petrol from the old -style 'Little David' pumps.

Over the years, there were a number of shop-assistants, but in the minds of many, the most striking individuals who actually owned the shop were, successively, Ashley Green and Mrs Ivy Spall.

Ashley Green was the last of the Green dynasty who owned the whole complex of shops and forge and dwellings, and lived next door in Forge House. He died at the end of World War II, leaving everything - shop and all - to Ivy and Arthur Spall who had been very good to him. The Spalls were living at The Plough and Ivy quickly rented out the shop. She told her first tenants, the Bowmans, who had always wanted a shop, that they could buy up the existing stock.

Other couples who managed the shop were: John and Margaret Lyon, a Mr and Mrs Pilgrim, and Margaret and David Oddy, who dealt with the changeover to decimalization. There were various assistants who came and went, such as Barbara Hambling and a Miss Templar.

*Mrs Margaret Oddy at the counter of the Wissett shop, now Beck Cottage, c1970.*

The Norrises were the most memorable managers of the shop. Brian and Pat Norris, who had a daughter, were hard-working people. Brian's younger brother, Richard, took over.

Ivy Spall, in 1952, had sold the premises next door - Forge House, the stables and the forge, but she kept the shop until she died in the mid 1990s, aged eighty-six. It was sold as a private residence to David King in 1997. So the last shop was gone. David, his father Terry the postman and other family members spent a year, working night and day, to renovate the place. Heaving out the buried petrol tank from the front and side yard by bulldozer and fork-lift truck took the best part of a Sunday.

## Forge House, No 32 The Street

In conjunction with wheelwrights and metal-forgers, there have been smiths in Wissett for centuries. There is a record of a ploughwright in 1600. We know definitely that the men who lived on this site during the 1800s were smiths; whether part of the forge was in this actual building is unclear. Certainly the west end was used for storage and stabling the horses before shoeing. It is more likely that the working forge was all contained in the adjacent building, now The Old Forge Cottage.

We know that the forge was worked by George Hufflett in the 1830s and 40s, with John Aldridge alongside him. A Henry Watson had joined Hufflett by 1844, while in 1858, the Green dynasty ran the whole enterprise.

Robert Green worked as blacksmith and wheelwright at the forge from 1858, and

65

*Walter Miller the blacksmith in the 1920s*

probably retired to No 18 The Street in 1883. He seems already to have handed over the running of the forge to his two relatives (nephews, most likely), John Oakley and George William Green. George was there for a remarkable fifty years - even John for a good thirty. George was joined by Walter Miller in about 1922. Walter lived over the road with his son Spider and daughter, Mrs Todd.

George and his brother John had come from the family's coach-building and blacksmith's business in Rumburgh. George died in 1936. Freddie Oxborough, who went to blow the organ at the funeral, said, 'I wish it was me in that coffin,' for like George he had cancer. Two weeks later, Freddie was dead too. Both were buried in Wissett churchyard. In 1940, George's widow Emma died and was buried beside her husband. Their son Ashley inherited the smithy and all the other buildings.

Ashley, with another relative, George A Green, hired out the forge until his death in 1947. He was only fifty-four or so, and died sitting in his chair, leaving the kettle boiling. It was a Saturday. Arthur Spall from The Plough went across eventually to see why Ashley wasn't around with his 'list,' for every Saturday Ashley used to do a bit of shopping for Arthur. It was Arthur who found him dead, and the Reverend John Cornell who officiated at his funeral.

By the early 1950s, Chris Minns was at the forge, working as the last smith. He came in from Halesworth. People remember him as a kind man who forged brass candlesticks for them as presents.

In 1952, Ivy Spall sold Forge House and the forge next door to George and Maud

Frost of Grove Farm. 'Wonky' Frost is remembered with affection as handing out Bluebird chocolate toffees to the schoolchildren in the 1950s.

Forge House with the adjacent forge was sold by Maud Emma Frost's executors in 1973 to Adrian Talbot, who moved in with his family of six or seven to the east end of Forge House. The west end was left as a stable where Adrian kept his horse, carriages, cars and oddments. The smithy (now The Old Forge Cottage) contained all the old implements that Adrian hoped one day could be got together again as a working forge.

Once, Adrian garaged a Rolls Royce car in his stables. Perhaps he was embellishing the number plates, for among his varied talents Adrian was a sign-writer. The Rolls belonged to the 'Ozzie' Earl ('call me Keith') of Stradbroke. The car emerged from the Talbot stables painted with Constable landscapes in hectic hues.

After Adrian, family in tow, left Wissett for France, Charlotte and Andrew Pringle bought Forge House in May 1993. They had been reassured that the Beck, which runs directly behind their house, never flooded. However, in the flood of 1994, Andrew remembers local people rowing down the street in dinghies. As the Reverend Derek Tilston observed, 'Wissett for a short time looked like a lovely village Venice!' Charlotte is an exquisite cook, while Andrew is an artist with a studio in Walberswick. They have a little daughter, Anabel.

For a year or two after they had bought Forge House, Charlotte continued in her job as cook to Lord and Lady Menuhin in Gstaad, Switzerland. Andrew was butler-cum-chauffeur. Every so often they arrived back in Wissett with many a tale of hard work and grandeur amidst the artistic high society of Europe.

## The Old Forge Cottage

This was all part of the forge complex, and actually where the anvil, furnace, bellows and other blacksmiths' equipment was situated. The horses were shod here, and cartwheels, farm implements of all descriptions as well as household utensils were repaired, fashioned or sharpened. Before Adrian Talbot sold this area, he donated all the smithy apparatus to Halesworth & District Museum, where it is now on display.

It was Geoff Abbott, builder, who bought this part of the forge in about 1991. He took three years to transform it into the studio home it now is. He then sold it to Lucy Hollis, a horsewoman. Lucy's father, the Reverend Tim Hollis, who had estates in Sotherton, leases it out. His present tenants at this cottage are Simon Ratcliffe and Carolyn Ashton, who play music and run the Wednesday night busking sessions at The Plough. Carolyn is a designer and architectural model-maker, and was in partnership with the late lamented Paul Lucas (once of Peartree Villa). A former partner was Alan Manton (once of Tudor Cottage).

## No 31 The Street *(formerly Blue Haws or Blue Haw Cottage)*

This cottage was only half its present size before Philip Lurkins bought it in 1989 and considerably modernized it, adding an extra wing for himself and his family: wife Maree, a hairstylist who also is a barmaid at the Spexhall Huntsman and Hounds Inn, and three sons: Jake(10), Jordan(8) and Travis(4). Phil handles his own building-contractors company.

During the nineteenth century, this little cottage was run as a small sub-post office. William Nunn, mentioned in the records from 1864 as 'Grocer' and 'Tailor' had taken charge of the post office from 1879, if not earlier. Kelly's Directory for 1894 lists William's widow, Mrs Harriet Nunn, as sub-postmistress here, where postal orders could be issued but not paid, the nearest 'money order and telegraph office' being in Halesworth (apparently in John Foreman's premises on the site of the present Midland Bank).

Mrs Dorothy Boast remembers a Mrs Kemp running Blue Haws post office. The letter-box was on the wall fronting the street, where now the figures '31' are. Dorothy next remembers Sid Johnson taking over when Mrs Kemp moved to No 7 The Street. Then it seems that Mrs Salmon took on the post office at No 18 The Street, while Sid Johnson and son retired from the business, and Blue Haws became a dwelling-place. For a while, George Hunting from No 3 The Street lived here after his wife Elsie died. Mrs Hammond, grandmother of Ron, and Harry Perry, who had run The Plough, also lived here at different times. One of the best-loved and well-remembered characters of the village who lived at Blue Haws all his working life until his death in 1977 was Jimmy Cutts, the chimney-sweep. He was only sixty-seven when he was buried in Wissett

*The forge, with the anvil, old-style bellows, and furnace. (Photo courtesy of Mike Fordham)*

churchyard, where he now shares a double headstone with his older brother, 'Fella,' who joined him in the grave in 1982.

Eric Stollery, who lives opposite No 31, remembers rescuing Jimmy from Blue Haws during the flood in 1976. Jimmy, a portly soul, was swung out by Eric on a rope across the flooded road, but was laughing so much that he fell in the murky waters, eventually reaching safety thoroughly drenched.

After Jimmy's time, Wonky Frost lived here for a while after his wife's death and sale of Forge House.

The cottage was eventually bought by Jill and Alistair Macfarlane and used as a holiday cottage, until Philip Lurkins bought it. Other members of Phil's family include his prize budgerigars, cockateels and pedigree springer spaniels that he breeds, and diverse pets.

## Saffron Cottage, No 29-30 The Street

The first reference to these two cottages is in 1828, when John and Rebecca Mayhew 'released' them to John Oldring of The Swan Inn. John Mayhew, a tailor, leased a blacksmith's shop and cottages at Holton from Mary Patterson in 1827.

In 1866, the cottages were sold to Joseph Berry, who by 1840 already owned Wissett forge, and occupied the old parsonage (the one before the present building) that was glebe land managed by the Reverend Francis Blick.

Much Beck water flowed under the bridge by these cottages before we next hear of them, at the turn of the nineteenth to twentieth century.

The left half of the cottage was occupied by the Taylor family, and the right half by the Cutts.

George ('Pod') Taylor was the son of George ('Pod') Hunter and a Miss Taylor, who married Pod Hunter after their son was born. She later 'got religion, Linstead way, put a cake in the oven, then went out and drowned herself in a pond.'

Her son, Pod Taylor, married Annie Oxborough and they lived most of their lives together at what was subsequently to be called Saffron Cottage, but at that time had no name and no key to the front door -'and no need of one,' says Elizabeth, Annie's middle daughter. When the three daughters were young in the 1920s and 30s and living in the left-hand cottage, Ted Cutts and his wife Ethel were on the other side with their six growing children: Wilfred, Harold ('Fella', because he was a tall fellow), and James ('Jimmy' the sweep, who lived at Blue Haws as a man), followed by Alice, Ethel and Madge. Elizabeth remembers being in her pram and Madge Cutts in hers, holding hands across the prams as their mothers wheeled them to Halesworth. Ted was an ingenious, diligent man. He kept a mule ('Muley') in the stables, now the garage, and had a smokehouse where he'd smoke kippers and sell them to the village, along with rabbits, chickens, pigs and ducks.

Never short of inventive ideas, Ted would buy crates of slightly scruffy chickens at auctions, spruce up their combs with his wife's lipstick, and sell them on at once.

The Taylor and Cutts younger children used to play to the left side of the cottages, by the Beck, where Phil Lurkins' bird-huts now stand. They would incur the wrath of Ashley Green, who lived with his parents in the forge house and owned the land by the Beck.

69

*Ted and Ethel Cutts with their children Harold, Wilfred, Alice and Jimmy outside Saffron Cottage, c1916*

All the children from both families went to the village school. Dora, the eldest Taylor daughter, had a Rudge Witworth bicycle, which was the height of smartness. Her sister Elizabeth says they were always quarrelling over it although when she was fourteen, Elizabeth earned £5 strawberry picking, and bought herself a Hercules bike. But it was no match for Dora's Rudge Witworth.

The skies were fairly empty in the years between the wars, so for an airship to fly over Wissett was an exciting, even a frightening event. Dora recalls the R101 airship coasting over Saffron Cottage from Calver's field behind the church in the early evening of 4 October 1930. Next day came the disastrous news of its crash near Beauvais.

The girls remember the earth tremor of 1931, centred off Dogger Bank. It was late on a Saturday night in early June, when everyone was in bed. Suddenly there was a huge roar and violent shaking. Annie and the girls rushed to the bedroom windows, to see Nurse Hilling opposite and all the villagers poking their heads out of their upper windows, gradually lighting their candles up and down the street. People were thrown out of bed; glasses and crockery smashed. In the morning, the young Cutts and Taylor girls ran to the enormous old chestnut tree, that had a bough-seat for them to swing on, by The Swan. Thankfully, they saw that their beloved tree was intact, and bursting into bloom.

After the war, when Elizabeth (now Mrs Davey) came back to Wissett to Sunnyside, she transplanted a tiny Scots pine from her garden there to Saffron Cottage where her mother Annie still lived. The pine stands now about thirty feet tall, by the Beck, to the left of the cottage. When the Cutts had moved and the Taylor girls were older, Margie, the youngest daughter, moved to the Cutts' half of the cottage next to her by now widowed mother. Margie married first Gerard Holland, an Irish soldier who fought in the Eighth Army, and after her divorce, Gerry Day. In 1967, Annie, Margie and Gerry moved into what had been the school, but was newly transformed into small homes.

Various members of the Bircham family of Westhall Hall had owned the cottages since the 1950s. They were sold in 1963 to James Potter Pianey of the White Horse, Baddingham. The big change to the appearance of Saffron Cottage happened in 1967, when Percy De'ath bought it. Percy, a Yorkshireman, and his wife Phyllis had moved from Saffron Walden, and named the cottage after that town.

When the stairs got too much for Phyllis, she and Percy moved over the road to No 21, and Saffron Cottage was sold to Alastair and Jill Macfarlane in 1975. Jill became very involved with the church and was a lay preacher, taking services on numerous occasions. Alastair's company, AMAC Boxes, was a finalist in the National Packaging Awards 2000. In his spare time as a model railway enthusiast, Alastair laid some forty yards of 'O' Gauge track in the front garden to accommodate his model steam trains. This was known as The Wissett Steam Railway, and used for charity fundraising. Alastair was chief sidesman at the church for several years, and responsible for hoisting the flags on various feast days, and maintaining the flagpole.

In August 1998, Jill and Alastair moved to Halesworth and the new owners of Saffron Cottage are the Wragg family: Michael, Tracey, Poppy (11), James (7), plus assorted grandparents.

## The Old Vicarage

Mr Kevin Nunn, born and bred in Wissett, has some very convincing theories about ancient sites in Wissett. He propounds that in the Middle Ages there was a theological college in the vicarage meadow, which is now part of The Old Vicarage. If so, it would have been connected with the Benedictine monks attached to the church. A note in the *Suffolk Parish History* tells us that in 1597 'the Parsonage house wants thatching.' This seems to be the first reference to an actual house for the parson. One can only surmise that as the church in 1602 was 'in a ruinous state' then the parsonage was likely to be too! We hear little of the 'perpetual curacy' other than that the curate in 1597 was the rebellious Mr Smyth (qv under The Clergy), that the curate's stipend was £13 6s 8d in 1603, and that the next named parson was a Mr Swallow, presumably living in the parsonage, who died in 1609.

Apart from the unverifiable almanac stating that the Wissett parsons lived for centuries at Box Farm, there seems to be no specially designated abode for clergymen in Wissett until the 1830s. An entry in the *Suffolk Parish History* for 1831 comments: 'No glebe house.' It is not known where the Reverend Edward Cornish Wells of Wissett lived then. The state of affairs changed with the Reverend Francis Blick, who managed glebe lands in Wissett in the 1830s and 40s. The new 'parsonage house' was built in 1843, at a

*The Old Vicarage in the year 2000*

cost of £700. Before that, according to the 1839-41 Tithe list, Joseph Berry (who owned the forge complex with Henry Birch) had lived in the old 'Vicarage, garden & co.' while William Hartopp was the 'impropriator'(a sort of lay landlord of ecclesiastical property) who collected tithes of £452 per annum. The incumbent of the new parsonage, The Reverend Robert Kemp, received a mere £90. The building became known as The Vicarage and Robert Kemp was there until at least 1875. Kemp was 'Vicar of Wissett and Walpole,' a man of extremely broad views and Christian outlook. On his way to Walpole church in his pony-drawn trap, he would regularly pick up the non-conformist minister of Walpole chapel, the Reverend Joseph Mayhew, (also a Wissett man) and deposit him at the rival place of worship. Kemp was followed by the Reverend Joseph Hindley in the early 1880s, the Reverend William George Baxter from 1885, and by the Reverend Henry Dunsterville Day in the 1890s. Dunsterville Day was also vicar of Dunwich, but resided in Wissett from 1895 as 'sequestrator' (according to Kelly's Directory) 'pro hac vice the Bishop of Norwich by lapse'! This presumably means that the church lands were making a loss and the vicarage could be repossessed. The Reverend Day was appointed to hold the property until claims against it were satisfied. It looks as if it were considered too expensive to run the vicarage AND give the incumbent a stipend. Nett values of glebe land and residence were depreciating rapidly, and more and more villagers were by now attending the non-conformist chapel at the other end of the village.

So by 1908, we find The Vicarage was occupied by a Miss Pennington. Henceforth, the Church of England clerics of Wissett resided at Spexhall. Mr Johnny Nunn reminds us that his Grandmother Nunn stayed at The Vicarage house for some time, before Mr Alfred Conrad Pawlyn. This gentleman was known affectionately as 'Tallin Paulin' (possibly due to his height), and was at The Vicarage during the First World War. His daughter, Christina, is now a hale octogenarian, and regularly visits her one-time nanny, Mrs Dorothy Boast. Dorothy, who lived in, laughs quietly as she remembers overhearing the workers walking past The Vicarage at the crack of dawn on their way to the farms: 'Look! the buggars aren't up yet!' one would exclaim, as he hitched his 'frail'(woven haversack on a stick) over his shoulder. 'De-ow (no) - they's got another couple o' hours yet!' the other would rejoin.

In 1928 the property was 'conveyed by the Incumbent of Wissett with the concurrence of the Ecclesiastical Commissioners to the late Mrs Harriet Howlett.' According to the directories, Thomas Howlett lived there at the beginning of the war. In 1942, The Vicarage, with vacant possession, was put up for sale by auction through the representatives of the late Mrs Harriet Howlett.

Previous to this, the meadow behind The Vicarage had belonged to Miss Florence Ewbank of Wissett Lodge. She had rented the meadow out to Charles Calver of Chediston Street, Halesworth. Charles was a fruit-and-vegetable market trader. Miss Ewbank died in 1915, leaving the meadow to Charles in her will. He moved two old railway carriages onto the meadow and lived there. He had six sons, four of whom served in the First World War. There were Hubert, Frank, Bertie, Philip, Lester and Roger. Bertie died during the war in France, only seventeen years old; Philip emigrated to Australia. When Charles died in 1927, he left the field to his eldest son Hubert. In 1938, Hubert's younger brothers, Lester (known as Hector, who had just married) and Roger, moved into the old railway carriages that were still there. In June of that year, these enterprising young brothers bought the field from Hubert for £170. Hector and Phyllis had three children, Sheila, Michael and Robin, in the carriages. Then, for about £1000 in December 1942, they bought The Vicarage House, where they moved in 1943. Four more children were born: Ray, Colin, Trevor and Ivan. The meadow at the rear was planted up with strawberries and is well remembered for the picking season and many a lovely ripe strawberry sampled. There was seasonal work for a great number of villagers in the orchards and packing sheds. Hector had a wonderful singing voice which, people recall nostalgically, floated across the strawberry fields and apple orchards:

> 'When shadows fall and trees whisper day is ending,
> My thoughts are for ever wending home,
> When lovebirds call, my heart is forever yearning
> Once more to be returning home.....'

This was always known as 'Hector's Song.'

By 1965, when all the children but Ray had 'flown the nest,' and Phyllis had died, Hector and Roger lived out their years together. Their deaths happened within a few weeks of each other in October and November 1993. The Vicarage was then sold to Michael Doherty and Mary Pester, who have done extensive work to the house and garden. Mary teaches at a primary school in Beccles while Michael is a tour director. Mary has become very involved in the village and organizes the flowers in the church.

## The Church

Three things of note about the church are its name, its position and its tower.

The name of the church, St Andrew's, Wissett, is appropriate, since Andrew was the patron of fishermen, and centuries of parishioners have been fishermen off the Suffolk coasts. The Saint's day, 30 November, is still celebrated here, and the churchwarden provides a fish supper for all after the service.

Whether, as some believe, the name 'Wissett' derives from the Norse *Veseti:* 'dwellers of the heathen temple,' or whether the name is from *withthe-geset:* 'withy beds,' both derivations could account for the church's low-lying position by water meadows and wooded groves; for it might have been built on the site of a small Celtic church, which favoured such spots over high ground above a village that the Normans chose. There used to be a ford where now Lodge Lane meets the main Wissett street at the bridge over the Beck.

Kevin Nunn (Sugar Nunn's grandson) puts forward an even more intriguing observation: that many of the churches in England dedicated to St Andrew are on non-Christian sites, and that the name 'St Andrew' is associated with 'Apollo.' Kevin quotes from *Timpson's Leylines* which suggests that 'the Romans identified St Andrew with the Celtic god Grannus and when early Christians built churches on sites where Grannus had been worshipped they dedicated them to St Andrew because the names sounded vaguely similar. Presumably they hoped the local pagans would not notice the difference.' Grannus was the god of mineral springs.

The most striking feature of the church is its round tower. Wissett is one of the forty-one round-towered churches still standing in north east Suffolk. It suggests a Saxon lookout tower against the marauding Danes. Cattle used to shelter in the ground floor part, and some say that there was an outside door facing westwards. Vestiges of double-splayed Saxon windows can be discerned if you climb up inside the tower, having got the key from Denis Simpson at Rose Cottage. It then becomes clear that the tower was originally much shorter, built in about 900 to between thirty-five and forty feet.

Apart from the round tower, the plan of the church is a simple rectangular nave and chancel, built largely from Suffolk flint. In *Suffolk Domesday* (William the Conqueror's census of 1086), one of the entries for Wissett reads thus: 'In the same Wissett 1 church, 2 carucates of free land.....5 villagers are attached to this church; 52 acres. 4¹/₂ ploughs. Meadow, 1 acre. In this church are 12 monks, and under it 1 chapel (capella).' A carucate was a measure of land as much as could be tilled with one plough in a year. The 'church' here is probably the Benedictine priory at Rumburgh (founded by Norfolk monks in 1064, and disbanded by Cardinal Wolsey for his college in Ipswich in about 1528), which fell within the parish of Wissett. So all told, the 'church' at Rumburgh plus its 'cell' in Wissett covered a sizeable acreage, although by 1340 it had shrunk to under a quarter of its original lands.

Many noteworthy features in this friendly little church are described in Margaret Kiddy's handbook, *St Andrew's, Wissett: a Guide*, well worth studying.

Here merely will be noted the pews, and the poppyheads saved from the original ones, the octagonal font supported by 'woodwoses' or reliefs of wild men and lions, the various memorials and escutcheons (re-painted by Walter Lamb in the 1970s), and the bier ('spelt "bier" not "beer",'said Mr Lewis Rowe at an Entertainments Committee meeting once).

*Wissett church, c 1970, after an etching by Anthony Dunigan*

*Walter Kerrison, one of the dedicated bell-ringers.*

The pews were renewed in 1843, and the pew list with its numbered seatings survives. The list starts at the top right side, facing the altar, with the vicar's pew at No 1, and Robert Tacon (of The Red House) and Richard Allen's pew at No 2, going down to the back of the church at No 16 and No 17, where the men and women servants would sit, and coming up to the other side of the aisle to William Hartopp's pew at No 30 (Lord of the Manor) for occupation by John Tillott (Manor agent at Wissett Lodge), and right at the top, opposite the vicar, the widows' pew at No 32!

Many hundreds of people of Wissett have helped to make the church what it is today, whether in their capacity as vicar, congregation, choir, bell-ringer, organist, treasurer, warden, flower-arranger, cleaner, carpenter, mason; or in their capacity as benefactor. One of the earliest men to give money to the church was John Aldrych, who left two marks 'to reparation of tower and other reassances,' in 1439. In 1453, William Sampson willed twenty shillings 'to high cross to be hung in Wissett Church.' Alice Potter left 3s 4d 'to priming of the font,' while the next year Robert Stall(ke) donated twenty shillings 'to painting of font.' We forget that stonework was painted, right through the ages from Ancient Egyptian times.

The cup is Elizabethan, while the two pewter plates are inscribed: 'The parish of Wissett in Suffolk 1713.' The Royal Coat of Arms was painted by T Rounce of Halesworth, as were the Lord's Prayer and the Ten Commandments, that hang on boards at the back of the nave, where the gallery used to be (for the choir and Sunday School girls). Radiators were donated by the Scrimgeours in the 1920s. The brass candlesticks fashioned by Chris Minns at the forge that shamefully were stolen were replaced by the beautiful Wissett oak ones  carved by Bill Ritchie. The organ was a gift from Marjorie Ballard and Lizzie Eagle Bott in 1968.

## The Church Bells

Of the six bells in the church tower, two are quite old, probably late medieval. One is thought to have been cast in Bristol between 1350 and 1380. Another is inscribed 'Virgo Maria' and has a wheel stop of the kind made by a London bellfounder, William Burford, whose will was dated 1390. A return of 1553 shows four bells, while by 1890 there were five. Three of the present bells were cast by Thomas Gardiner of Benhall, near Saxmundham, in 1718, and another was cast by T Mears of London in 1818. The newest treble bell came from A Bowell of Ipswich, and was dedicated on 9 October 1910. Up until 1976, when the wooden bell frame was declared too weak to tolerate the vibrations from ringing the changes, there had been great feats of ringing for centuries.

One of the legendary ringers of Wissett from the 1880s was Charles Kerrison, who would ring one bell in each hand and work another with a foot. His son Walter remembered that as a little boy in about 1890 he used to pull the left hand for his father. Walter became a dedicated ringer, and joined the North East Branch of the Suffolk Guild of Ringers. He taught half a dozen would-be campanologists, his most astonishing pupil being a sixteen-year-old girl from Spexhall who speedily acquired the art of ringing four bells while still having a finger to spare to take over the conducting. The bells were pealed on state occasions no less than local ones. Queen Victoria's Golden Jubilee in 1887, The Coronation of King George V in 1911, Victory Day in 1945, Prince Charles' birth in 1948 were all commemorated by the Wissett bell-ringers. Miss Patricia Stanford recalls that her mother, Ione Bunbury, and her aunt, Vera Bunbury, when they both lived at Willow Grange used to be part of the village bell-ringing team. In 1911, the Rector's sister Miss Garforth became the first woman to 'achieve a peal of Bob Minor' on the Wissett ring of bells.

A big achievement was the 1951 quarter peal of Grandsire Doubles (1260 changes) rung in forty-six minutes for the ringer of the Third, upon his joining HM Forces. The ringer of the Third was young Robert Moore, and the rest of the team were: C Aldridge - Treble; Walter Kerrison - Second; J Jordan - Fourth; R Darch - Fifth (conductor); R Aldridge - Tenor.

*Wissett
Bell-ringers
1908-1910*

## The Clergy

The history of priests, priors, curates, vicars and others in charge of their flock in Wissett is long and quite difficult to reconstruct.

From Saxon times, there were many powerful centres of worship under the Bishopric of East Anglia, particularly the Abbey of St Edmundsbury, which contained the shrine of the martyred Saxon King. No less in this part of north east Suffolk, there was the great moated Minister of South Elmham, and many monastic houses which grew in importance after the Conquest, such as the Benedictines, Dominicans and Franciscans at Dunwich, and the Cistercians at Sibton.

On a smaller scale were the thatched churches or 'cells' with round towers at Wissett, Holton, Spexhall, Bramfield, and the church on the site of St Mary's Halesworth, which was, by the time of Domesday survey, under Ulf the priest. Wissett was under the spiritual guidance of the Benedictine Prior at Rumburgh, but by 1130, for the first time a curate is named: William de Wysete. The curates must have worked alongside the abbots and priors, for even by 1340 Wissett was not independent of the monastic houses. Records in the fourteenth century include Wissett church as having fifty-five acres and as being part of Sibton Abbey, near Walpole, which was Cistercian. It is not clear if Wissett had changed spiritual allegiance from Benedictine to Cistercian.

It appears that Wissett church came under the manor of Le Roos in about 1499, and in the following century are records of individual clerics - of varied character and talents. In 1539, Sir William Hall left money 'to common light,' while in 1597, there was a complaint about the curate, Mr Smyth, because he failed to wear the surplice, hold monthly sermons, or catechize the youth. The next named vicar is Mr Swallow, who died in 1609: there exists a letter from certain villagers of Wissett to a Sir Nathaniel Bacon, written on 10 June 1606, objecting to Bacon's choice of new vicar. The villagers wanted the late Reverend Swallow's brother, who was a 'teacher of singinge and musike,' to take over.

Apart from the mention of Robert More, churchwarden in 1718, there seems to be no ready record of any clergy until the Reverend Francis Blick, who managed glebe lands in Wissett in the 1830s and 40s; the Reverend Edward Cornish Wells (mentioned in Pigot & Co's Directory for 1830 as being of Wissett), the Reverend Richard Crutwell, rector of Spexhall in the 1820s and 30s, who owned No 18 the Street, Wissett, but whose interest in Wissett appears to have been financial and not spiritual, and the Reverend Robert Kemp, for whom the new 'parsonage' was built in 1843. Kemp remained until at least 1875. He was followed by the Reverend Joseph Hindley in the 1880s, and by the Reverend Henry Dunsterville Day and the Reverend William George Baxter in the 1890s. Dunsterville Day was also the vicar of Dunwich, but resided in Wissett from 1895 as 'sequestrator.'

For economic reasons, the living of Wissett was joined with that of Spexhall. The first rector to hold both livings was the Reverend John Garforth, who was the rector of Spexhall from 1882, adding Wissett in 1912. The next rector of the combined benefice was John Hughes in 1916, followed by Arthur Trousdale in 1929. By now Wissett had settled into its new position as part of the diocese of St Edmondsbury, whereas up until Garforth's time it had been under the diocese of Norwich. The Reverend Trousdale was often discovered drinking in Southwold, but he could be a strict disciplinarian when someone's attention strayed in church. He was known to have stopped in mid-sermon to thunder at a small choir-girl, who was only reading the next hymn, 'Little girl! Will you please put that book down and listen to what I am saying! Remember that you are in the house of God!'

Arthur Trousdale was succeeded by the Reverend Charles R Heard in 1941. Three of the next four incumbents are all mentioned in Lizzie Eagle Bott's book, *I Looked Over The Gate.* The Reverend Cornell was a kindly person , who coached children for examinations, and had a son who caught meningitis when he was only two. The Reverend James Mortimer Lafontaine McNally is glossed over, but his successor, the Reverend Alan Watson, was the rector who inspired Lizzie Eagle Bott to play the organ in church, even though Lizzie was fifty-seven and had only just started learning. By 1963, Lizzie was playing the organ well enough to accompany the Confirmation Service for fourteen local candidates, in Wissett church, conducted by the Bishop of Dunwich, the Right Reverend T Cashmore. The next rector, who arrived in 1970, was the Reverend Norman Lifton. He was 'always drinking with the British Legion,' say those that know. He had a great big dog that was in the habit of brushing everything off the table when Norman visited. It was with him that Lizzie used to argue over the timing of the organ and the hymns.

In 1977 Wissett became part of Halesworth Team Ministry, which currently comprises eleven parishes. About this time, the Reverend Michael Woods appeared. He came from a family of Yarmouth boat-builders, and used to harbour all sorts of down-and-outs in his rectory at Spexhall. 'He should be looking after us, his parishioners!' Lizzie Eagle Bott would exclaim. 'I suppose he is, in his own way,' came the reply. He ran a youth club in the village hall, and is now a canon in Great Yarmouth.

In the 1980s, the Reverend John Kinchin-Smith was considered a kindly rector, good at pastoral visiting, and known affectionately as Rev Kitchen Sink. Daphne Ritchie, quite an adept at palmistry, recalls a certain church fête, where she was busy in a marquee ('which,' says Daphne, 'had the longest queue') reading people's palms in the most harmless of ways. Nevertheless, Daphne received a visitation at her home one day from the Reverend Kinchin-Smith to inform her that reading palms was not a suitable activity for a church fund-raising event. Daphne's mild protestations fell on deaf and rather stuffy ears.

After the departure of the suffragan Bishop Tim of Dunwich, a new suffragan bishop was created, Bishop Clive of Dunwich, while Bishop Richard Lewis remained Bishop of St Edmundsbury. The Reverend Tony Norton was appointed to the rectory of Spexhall in 1996, from where he oversees many activities within the two linked parishes. As well as the more usual services, Tony leads the walk round the farms and the blessing of the crops and livestock on Rogation Sunday, the Clipping of Wissett church on Shrove Tuesday, the Carrying of the Cross up the Green Hill on Good Friday, and other rituals ancient and modern. Although the Team lost its enterprising Team rector, Leonard Doolan, in 1998, it has gained the Reverend Mary Joel, who used to live at The Pines before she was priested, and who now travels in to Wissett every week, and with tireless dedication has inspired a number of innovations within the church ministry, particularly with the children.

## The Village Hall

The buildings on this site over the last hundred and fifty years have included a dwelling house, three schools and a village community centre,

In the 1830s, according to the Tithe map, a cottage and garden stood here, known as the Vicarage Cottage, let out to James Jackson and partner. It was glebe land managed by the Reverend Francis Blick. In the Public Record Office at Kew, there exists an indenture of 1845 for an agreement for the use of this cottage as a school (a National Society Church of England School), between the Reverend Robert Kemp, Perpetual Curate of Wissett, and Edward, Bishop of Norwich. An affidavit was signed by three other clergymen to check Kemp was up to running a school! The signatures were witnessed by John Phillips, the benevolent non-conformist businessman.

The school was obviously set up, but teaching had gone on in the village some years before Vicarage Cottage was turned into a school building. Prior to the Reverend Kemp, Lucy Davy had been the village schoolteacher, and in 1844 Robert Cooper was paid 15s for the use of his house as a schoolroom up till Michaelmas. Quite separately, a Church of England Sunday School is listed as having been established in 1818, with thirty attending, and thirty-five attending in 1833.

After the founding of the National Society Church of England school in 1845, we do not know what happened to the Reverend Kemp or Miss Davy, but we do know that James Self became master of the new school in 1858, with Mrs Self assisting, and that Mrs Sarah Algar (whose husband ran the shop at No 18 The Street) became mistress in 1875. A School Board was established on 27 September 1878, with five members. There was an average of sixty-five children that year. However, the first entry in the Wissett Board School log books is not until April 1879, and reads as follows:

'The School was opened on 14th April 1879. It is under the management of a School Board consisting of the following members: Mr C Smith (Chairman), Messrs A Blundell, W Bishop, F Chambers, G Maelal(sic) Keep (Clerk to the Board).'

The first teacher under this new system was Julia C Luthman, and sixteen boys and sixteen girls were admitted. The attendance was erratic and on 4 July of that same year Julia Luthman resigned and the school closed.

Another attempt to get the school underway was made almost immediately. Mrs Sarah Algar, who had already tried her hand at school teaching in 1875 under the old system, opened the school again on 8 July with sixteen pupils. But on the 5 September Sarah wrote in the log book: ' The school will be closed today on account of the harvest.' She had presumably had enough, because no more is heard of her at the school.

In October 1879 the Board School opened for the third time, with Christina Blyth as the main schoolmistress and Emily Elsom arriving to help her in 1881. The premises were rented from the vicar, and would hold seventy children. Arrangements were made for harvest holidays, Christmas and Easter. In 1883 Miss Blyth resigned and Miss Elsom took over as senior mistress.

In May 1880, a scale of pay was fixed by the Board: 1d per week for a child under seven and 1d for Juniors; 2d for the senior children over seven in a family. Although the school received a grant from the Government, in 1891 the grant of £17 8s 4d was cut by a tenth because the Inspectors' Annual Report was critical of the work - particularly the embroidery! - and organization of the school (even though approval was given to the teachers and pupils).

*Wissett Church Nativity Play c1970s. Among the children are, from the back: Francis Middleton-Stewart, Teresa Wing, Maureen Hunt, Stephen Oddy, Miss Eagle Bott, Angela Reeder, Robert Oddy, Reverend Lifton, Caroline Lawrence, Julie Whistlecraft, Ross Addison-Carter, Sadie Wing, Mark Whistlecraft and Gregory Nicholls.*

By now the Reverend M Hindley, Dr Pedgrift and Mr Settling were on the School Board, which met once a month at the King's Arms Hotel in Halesworth. A new school building replaced the old one in 1884, for fifty pupils. Things seemed to be improving. Selina Shelter (or Shelton) came to teach in 1888 and had two monitors: Annie Allen and Annie Hurren, previous pupils.

In September 1890 Kate H Green became the mistress, and the school continued to evolve, in spite of a few setbacks by way of disease - smallpox, diphtheria, whooping cough and influenza. For instance the school had to close in November 1893 owing to two deaths from diphtheria.

In 1894, the last hiccup occurred: Kate Green resigned on 22 June; a Mr Charles Wood started teaching on 25 June, but on 19 October he resigned. Finally, Thomas Cooper Ollis became head teacher on 19 November 1894. Mr Ollis used to walk to school from the Rumburgh end of Gray's Lane, and, the stories go, was a fitting target for his odd behaviour. He would hide in the hedgerow from any children who came to waylay him. In due course, the children would give up waiting to pounce on the poor man, and dawdle down to school. They invariably arrived late, and would be caned for being so by the miraculously-appearing Mr Ollis. Another trick he had was to produce an orange, peel it and ask, 'Who likes oranges?' The pupils would chorus, 'I do!' to which Mr Ollis would rejoin, 'Then see me eat it!'

Apart from these minor episodes, we may assume all went well. A new School Board of five members convened, with John Oakley Green as clerk to the Board, and we hear no more of school upheavals until 1908, when the village hall stopped functioning as a school, and the new council school was built on the outskirts of Wissett (now the School Bungalows).

The village hall from 1908 was given over to the community for use. Within living memory, the hall was divided into two during the 1920s: the Club room and the Sunday School room. The Club room had a billiards table, among other facilities, and piles of old 'Punch' magazines, donated by Marjorie Scrimgeour. Freddie Oxborough was caretaker, and saw to the old 'tortoise' stoves, one in each room. These stoves were the round cast-iron sort, with flues up the centre, and fed with coal from the coal-shed outside the hall.

During the war, the hall was used by the Home Guard for training. It was on one such training exercise that Poodle Cutts accidentally dropped his gun and it went off, shooting a hole in the ceiling. Many changes have taken place over the last seventy years; many a committee has sat in the hall; many suppers, feasts, shows, Women's Institute meetings, displays, art workshops, fund-raising sales and events such as bowls matches. Colonel Tomkin was chairman of the Wissett Village Hall Committee when it was established as a charity in the 1970s. The hall underwent major refurbishment at the same time and again in the mid 1990s, when an extension was added on. David Andrews succeeded Mike Tomkin as Village Hall Committee chairman. Eric Stollery is the caretaker today and has painted the hall numerous times.

*Eddie Cutts and Eva Gardiner's Wedding, with Madge, Ethel and Alice Cutts among the bridesmaids. Eddie was the oldest son of Ted Cutts by his first wife. Eva came from Bungay.*

*No 25 The Street*

*Village 'stir up' by WI President Claire Kiddy and Team*

*'Mayflower' (once The Old School)*

*The Wisdom Family*

*John Howlett*

*Brook Hall Farm*

*Grove Farm House*

*Ash Tree Farm*

*Halleluia Cottage in the snow*

*Whitehouse Farm*

*Gray's Lane in winter*

*Lodge Barn before conversion*

*Wissett Grange*

## Wissett Grange

This fine, timber-framed, listed building is probably fourteenth century. The sequencing of rooms suggests a mediaeval hall-house - the east end being the parlour with upper storey living space; the north end being service rooms with storage above. There might be a case for linking The Grange with the Benedictine Priory at Rumburgh. Alternatively, it could have been a small farmhouse run by lay brothers with allegiance to the pastoral Cistercians at Sibton Abbey.

However, the present owner, the barrister Mrs Caroline Burton, writes: 'There is no evidence whatsoever to connect The Grange to the Abbey' (ie Rumburgh) 'since the names of the land it owned are known.' Mrs Burton continues: 'So it seems that The Grange was never a religious building, but was always firmly in secular hands.....the house was always 'copyhold' land....once owned by the manor of Wissett Le Roos; every time the house was bought, sold or mortgaged, the transaction had to be done with the permission of the lord of the manor, given at the manorial court, in return for a fee paid to the lord, each transaction being recorded in the manorial rolls for Wissett Manor....We know from the court rolls that the farm was called Myrelds....In 1327, a tax was collected by Edward II to pay for the crusades, and in the village of Wissett, two shillings was paid by Johanna Myrel, after whom the house must have been named. Nothing is known about Johanna Myrel. However in about 1470 the simple mediaeval hall house was extended in an easterly direction, by an unknown individual who nevertheless was a man of wealth and skill....He may have been a master carpenter, because the massive new fireplace in the hall room contains on the bressumer a central badge of two crossed adzes. The ground floor room he built contains religious carvings on the supports to the ceiling beams.' These were very similar to the fifteenth-century emblems of the Passion (crown of thorns, nails, hammer and pincers, bleeding heart) found in the spandrels of Wissett church south porch by the great diocesan surveyor, Munro Cautley, in 1937.

The following centuries saw many alterations and room-divisions. Mrs Burton writes: 'In the early seventeenth century, the hall was further updated, by the addition of oak panelling with a frieze of carved dragons. Some of these improvements may have been done by the three generations of the Mighells family, who held the house from sometime in the sixteenth century to 1668. The Mighells were merchants in Lowestoft with numerous commercial interests in shipping trade and property. The Grange then passed to a widow, Mary Parker of Holton, her daughter Mary, who married into the Pallant family, and their descendants. Samuel Pallant married Elizabeth Pallant in Mendham church in 1713, and they set up home together at The Grange, selling in 1734.'

The Garrould dynasty of Spexhall, who farmed the area for hundreds of years, gave their name to two of The Grange and Manor fields, and by the 1830s, The Grange was part of the estate of Henry Bence Bence, Lord of Thorington Hall. Thorington churchyard is studded with memorials by the Bences to the worth and affection of their faithful retainers, some of whom served their whole life with the family. One headstone reads: 'In memory of John Walker, late of Wissett, died May 5 1878, aged 85 years.' Together with his parents, Margaret and John Walker, and many other family members, he farmed at Wissett Grange and Manor Farm over a lifetime.

By then The Grange was three tenement cottages, and at the turn of the century saw several different owners, including the dashing Colonel Harry Lake of The Red House, who had served in Austria, Turkey and Persia, crossed Siberia five times, mapped most of Johore, 'and seen Chinese pirates gobbling up their last grains of rice before being beheaded.' In the early twentieth century Herbert 'one-eyed' Broom (better known as developer of Holton Mill and Wissett Hall) briefly invested in the place before selling in 1909. The Grange was then 'restored and converted out of three cottages' (according to Norman Scarfe, vice-president of the Suffolk Institute of Archaeology and History) by the artist and designer John Seymour Lucas of Priory Place, Blythburgh, whose main claim to fame was a painting called *Flirtation* hung at the Guildhall, London.

During the years before the First World War, the walls of The Grange rang with society parties, as some of the gardeners and servants still in the vicinity remember. Miss Ewbank, who owned Wissett Lodge, was seen frequently here at The Grange, until her death in 1915. The Grange was then occupied by a Mrs Cussen, with Frederick William Leach as farm manager.

Around 1918, Miss Login retired here. Miss Login was the daughter of Lady Lena Login and Sir John Login (native of Orkney and one-time doctor in the Bengal Army) who had been 'superintendent' to Maharajah Duleep Singh, the tragic exile who in 1893 was buried ( a last insult, as he should have been cremated) at his seat at Elveden Hall near Thetford. Miss Login had a dog called Rover, 'a big ginger collie thing.' Bob Kerrison and his father Walter, of Nos 16-17 The Street, used to work for Miss Login, 'a plumpish, kindly figure in her fur coat.' When she was away, Bob and Walter would walk up to The Grange to check the greenhouses were warm enough and the oil-stoves lit. They would have Rover to stay with them in their tiny cottages throughout Miss Login's absence. The Reverend John Hughes presided over the funeral service for Miss Login in

Wissett church in 1927. She was seventy-two.

Her successor at The Grange was Frederick Herbert Watson, but for a short time only, for by 1930 the owners were the Goldspinks. They became very active supporters of the community. George Herman Goldspink was a loyal patron of the local cricket, football and rifle clubs, and among many other distinguished positions was chairman of the parish council. At the onset of World War II, he was deputy chief air-raid warden for the district. However, he shot himself on 21 November 1939. Some villagers aver that it was because he was so appalled by Hitler's inhumanity. He was only thiry-five. It was Ernie Mills the butler who found his body in the woods: 'Ernie whose wife married two brothers: Ernie was the second. They lived in the wooden bungalow up the steps on the mound to the left of The Grange.'

Mrs Goldspink Goldspink (double barrelled because her mother was a Goldspink as well as her husband) bravely carried on the good works of her husband. Until her death in 1965, she was a tireless administrator and the first woman chairman of Wainford rural district council, and held the office right up until the month before she died. At her funeral in Wissett, Lizzie Eagle Bott was the organist, and the Reverend Alan Watson conducted the service at which many distinguished mourners were present. 'She died of cancer,' reminisced a neighbour. 'She smoked seventy Goldflake a day.'

Wissett Grange in the 1970s was home to the Overburys; and then, in 1978, when the asking price was £47,500, it was bought by George Neocleous. From 1983 to 1994, Val and David Sawyer owned the place and undertook major refurbishments, including the chimneys and the roof, which they had rethatched by David Thompson. David Sawyer is a chartered surveyor and Val a committed member of the village Women's Institute.

The current owners are the barristers Caroline and Frank Burton QC with their three children: Dan, Tom and Tamar, who have come from London. They have been industriously continuing to restore The Grange 'to something of its original mediaeval simplicity.'

## Pine Lodge

This relatively new house was built in 1987 by Bernard and Angie Bremner. It replaces the Grange Bungalow which went with Wissett Grange and was the home of Mrs Goldspink's gardener, Ernest Harry Mills, and his wife Gertrude. Mrs Goldspink willed this bungalow to Jean Mary Gowing, a distant relative, and upon Mrs Goldspink's death in 1965, Ernie and Gertie Mills moved away.

John and Gillian Young are the new owners of Pine Lodge, having bought it from the Bremners in September 1999. They came from Maidstone in Kent and are planning extensions to their new home in the near future.

## Stone Cottage

This old cottage was built circa 1750 although its history is scant until the 1841 Tithe records, which show that it was owned by Charles Woodyard and occupied by 'John Manning and others.' Most people now remember it as two cottages: the right hand had been where the Cutts family lived; the left where Nellie and Freddie Oxborough lived for a while.

Poodle Cutts moved into Stone Cottage with his growing family in the early years of the twentieth century. He worked at Halesworth maltings and is remembered as a tall man, who lived till he was ninety. He married Alice Howlett from Harleston, and with her bought up ten children: Lily, Alan, Millie, Alfonso (Fonny), Stanley, Willie, Basil, Olive, Nelson and Peter ( who lives at No 6 Brickhill Cottages). Lily grew up and started work as a maid for Miss Login at Wissett Grange, before marrying and emigrating to Australia. Millie worked at Valley Farm and married Jim Ingate. Poor little Nelson, aged four, drowned in the Beck behind Stone Cottage; Stanley worked for many years as head gardener for the Calverts at Spexhall Manor, and Willie and Fonny are in Halesworth.

Willie, now eighty-eight, remembers his mother at the old Dutch oven, where she baked all her own bread. Every so often, the chimneys got blocked, so Poodle opened three gun cartridges and emptied the gunpowder into a bag. He'd throw the bag into the grate below the oven, strike a match, and shout at everyone: 'Stand back!' Willie and all used to cower and wait for the bang; and the soot flew out of the chimney - down and out as much as up!

Alice was apparently scared of dogs. On her walks to Rumburgh to visit her husband's sister, known as Aunt Mabel, she'd take a string of sausages. Whenever one of the farm dogs came 'worritting' her, she'd throw a sausage behind her, hoping to distract the animal. Of course, it came back for more, so the hapless lady progressed to Rumburgh a few paces at a time, interspersed with much strewing of sausages.

In the other half of the cottage, the Oxborough children were growing up: William, who later moved up to Mill Road and became father-in-law to Sid Aldridge at The Swan; Eliza, who subsequently had a daughter Millie; Charlie, who moved to Long Melford; Bertie who died young, and Annie, who married Pod Taylor and remained in Wissett. When the Oxboroughs left Stone Cottage, the Sadds arrived. Mr Tom ('Sooty') Sadd was gardener to Lewis Parry at Ash Tree Farm and Mrs Sadd was a domestic. Apparently Mrs Sadd once gave one of the local girls a piece of currant cake.

'It tasted like ferrets,' the girl told her mother.

'Have you ever tasted ferrets?'

'It tasted like ferrets smell!'

Tom Sadd died in 1943, and his wife had gone too; Alice and Poodle Cutts had moved to Brickhill Cottages by 1945. The new inhabitants were Alice Tricker and Gladys Ward. Alice Richardson retired here soon after she had sold The Pines in 1968. The cottages were modernized and made into a single dwelling. The next owners we know of are Jane and David Baxter who were here for about five years, succeeded by Mr and Mrs Finch.The current owners, Boris and Sylvia Faulconbridge, bought the cottage in 1998, having come from Walberswick.

*John and Emily Jordan at Wissett House.*

## Wissett House

The present owners, Louise and Julian Harris, were told this cottage was built in about 1780, because the walls had flint inner skin and brick outside. There were two bread ovens, one at either end, for it was two cottages then. By the 1840s, John Foyster owned the house and its plot or 'pightle,' while William Taylor lived there. A pightle is a relic from the days when elongated slips of land were left down the edge of a field after it had been divided for strip cultivation.

By 1912, a police officer is listed in the village. He probably lived in this cottage, for it was the Police House by 1925, when Police Constable Robert D Pearce is named as living here, with his wife and two children, Bob and Queenie. It was PC Pearce who tried to rescue little Kenny Debenham when he was knocked down near the school, and drove his mother and him to Halesworth hospital. It was also poor PC Pearce who was called to pull little Nelson Cutts out of the Beck where his brother Willie found him drowned. Mrs Alice Cutts at Stone Cottage used to see Mr Pearce passing by. If it was very early, she'd say, 'There goes Mr Pearce - I expect there's a birch on this morning,' for Mr Pearce administered birchings as punishments. The last boy he birched had thrown a big stone from 'Bungay Arch' at Halesworth and hit a train travelling on the railway lines below. Long afterwards, Mr Pearce was found hanged in his shed at Bungay. Lamentably, it seems that he was traumatized by more tragedies than he could bear.

After PC Pearce, PC William Thompson moved in with his wife, son Billy, and three daughters: Cissy, Hilda and Ellen.

Some of the ladies who were pupils then at the school next door remember the very day that the Thompsons arrived. Ellen was sitting on the dividing wall in a red jumper and navy-blue velvet skirt. She was dark and very beautiful. When she was older, and courting the handsome PC Finch, she used to 'ride through Wissett sitting on the cross-bar' of his bicycle. They had their wedding reception in the village school, and although they lived in Rendham for many years, PC Charles William Finch is buried in Wissett churchyard. Hilda too married a policeman: PC Walter James Pryke, in April 1934 in Wissett. Billy later married Marjorie (Joyce) Limmer at St Peter's Holton.

After the war, John and Emily Jordan arrived in the cottage. John worked for Mr Richardson at The Pines and was a Special Constable. John was known to help people with their gardens (Miss Eagle Bott's for one). On John's death, Emily was left with her much-loved dogs for company. She became a great help to Alice Richardson who moved into Stone Cottage next door. Emily was a dedicated chronicler, and it is thanks to her that we have so many cuttings and pictures of daily events within the parish. Moreover she was an exquisite needlewoman, and embroidered the altar cloth for the church.

The school playing field used to stretch right up to her front door, so she negotiated with the council, and bought some of the playing field, which was to the west, and sold a bit of her garden, which was to the east, to Stone Cottage.

Emily was an excellent gardener for many years, but as she grew older, she could no longer manage her plot. One day, in the early eighties, she was found weeping in the garden by Peter Cutts and Ernie Woolnough's brother, Clifford, who used to help her. 'I can't weed it any more,' she sighed. She knew she would have to move to a more manageable place, but it was not easy. When she finally had the cottage on the market in 1986, and had accepted Louise Harris's offer, the estate agent allowed someone else to put in a higher bid. But Emily was a woman of her word, and refused the late bidder.

Louise, from Earls Colne near Colchester, kept in touch with Emily for many years after Emily had moved to Halesworth. One day Lizzie Eagle Bott, who was very fond of Emily, came marching over to Louise and said, 'You'll have to move! Emily wants to come back!' But kind-hearted Louise found out that Emily was set on staying where she was. Emily died peacefully on Christmas Day 1992, asleep in her chair.

The cottage was in quite some disrepair, so Louise and her family set to. They discovered the porch had been made from a four-poster bed and the wood had become very rotten, so had to be dismantled. The walls, in spite of the original flint, were so damp that when Louise removed the wallpaper, the walls came down with it.

When Julian, Louise's husband, came to bulldoze and level out the overgrown wilderness, he discovered hundreds of Victorian bottles buried down near the Beck, which borders their property. This was normal practice: to bury one's waste. Now the cottage is transformed and the garden is landscaped with herb gardens, ponds, bowers, wooded areas, sweet-smelling shrubs and roses. There is an exciting play area for the children: Joanne(13) at Bungay High School; Michael (12) at Halesworth Middle School, and Debbie (8) at Edgar Sewter Primary School, Halesworth.

## The Old Schoolhouse, now known as Nos 1, 2 & 3, School Bungalows

On land owned by Henry Bence in the 1830s, known as Brook Pightle, this whole building was designed and built in 1908 as the new council school.

Originally there was one room, divided by a high partition, with the smaller part at the Wissett end for infants, and the larger Rumburgh end for juniors. There was an outside pair of bucket lavatories - on the Beck side.

The fortunes of this school over its half century of existence, and the various teachers with their differing and sometimes questionable skills, could easily fill another book, but to list only their names hardly does them justice.

Miss Alice S Branford was the first headmistress of the new school, with Miss Grace Young as infant teacher. By 1925, a Miss Doris Smith was in charge, and then Miss Gertie Aldred, whose younger sister Florrie also taught at the school. These are the first teachers to be remembered by people still in the neighbourhood today, such as Gertie and Florrie's sister, Mrs Dorothy Boast, and Mrs Ivy Cullingford (née Block). Then there was Miss Dolly Harold, and Miss Howell or Hole, who insisted on the children writing their address not as 'The' Street, Wissett, but as 'Wissett' Street, Wissett. One of her pupils, Dora Taylor (now Mrs Warren) in the 1930s won a scholarship to the Pupil-Teacher Centre (where now the Edgar Sewter School stands).

Miss Ballard was the next memorable teacher, initially Nurse Hilling's lodger at St Peter's Farmhouse. Another favourite was Miss Hardy, who gave every child apples from her pockets. This was wartime, and some children did not get any breakfast. Dinners came in from Beccles. There were several children evacuated to Wissett from Dagenham; some were entitled to council bicycles.

In the 1950s, when the Beck was frozen over, the boys in the village would slide to

*Wissett School c1930: Back Row - Miss Howell, Violet Aldous, Pinto Reeder, Roly Meen, Freddie Mouser, Leonard Block, Kenny Meen, Elizabeth Taylor, Mary Balls. Front Row - Maurice Godbold, Donald Meen, Madge Cutts, Marjorie Taylor, Doreen Foster, Olive Reeder, Olive (Florrie) Cutts, Lawrence Debenham, Stanley Aldous.*

school along the Beck, having to duck low under the bridge that used to span the Beck by the church. If they were sliding too fast, they'd crack their heads against the bridge, because the water level was much higher forty years ago.

Ray Calver can remember his teacher Miss Howard, who provided little plots for each child to create a garden.The last few years of the school's life in the mid-fifties saw the arrival of Miss Salmon from Walpole, and Miss Brenda Alden, who was, by all accounts, a breath of fresh air. She was young, vibrant, a good artist, and inspired the children with creative events - school plays, pageants, dance displays, outings and festivals.

Sadly, no teacher following Brenda could match her spirit. Miss Jackson was one of the last heads and is remembered for her strange antics: she apparently used to jump about in 'a sort of skating skirt,' getting the girls to be bunnies round the playground, to their embarrassment, as they were visible to the farmworkers on the road.

In the final year, there was a teacher Tony Willis remembers. Tony, aged about ten, was new to the school just before it was due for closure in 1961. The teacher, who was learning to drive, was so busy reading up her highway code and smoking on the apple tree stump in the yard that she regularly forgot her class. The situation was narrowly saved from chaos, says Peter Fleming, by his sister Beryl (McMorran) then aged about eleven, being able to help and organize the younger children who instinctively turned to her in their teacher's absence, or absent-mindedness!

The bolt was shot in 1961, when only a handful of children remained. The council converted the building into three small dwellings, and the first residents were Mrs Annie Taylor in one of them, and her daughter Margie with her husband Gerry Day next door.

*Wissett School 1948-49: Back Row - Ros Merryweather, Michael Calver, Ducha Matthews, Colin Gower, Josephine Evans, Miss Fanny Howard. Third Row - Jacqueline Maulden, Brian Sayer, Gloria Davey, Tony Aldridge, Alan Reeder, Sheila Calver, Alan Hall, Gillian Storey. Second Row - Ruth Goddard, Ray Calver, Geraldine Holland, Jean Nunn, Janet Hadingham, David Spall. Front Row - Sarah Nunn, Ivan Cutts, Pearl Ingate, Pat Aldridge and Robin Calver.*

Annie and Gerry both died in 1971, and unfortunately Margie started to ail. She was ill for a long time, looked after by her companion Guy Jolly, a thatcher, until the end, which came in 1989. Julian Harris remembers Margie as the gentlest of souls, the only person he has buried in Wissett churchyard, although he has buried other people in neighbouring village graveyards.

The third dwelling was occupied first by a Miss Turner, who, although almost blind, was a great companion to Annie Taylor. Miss Lizzie Eagle Bott told her: ' You made Mrs Taylor's last years very happy.' Then Fred Denmark and his second wife moved here from No 9 The Street. When Annie died, Fred moved into her part in the back 'west end,' and Arthur Borrett moved into the front where Fred had been. Eventually, in February 1996, Jack and Sheila Whitbread from Earls Colne near Colchester bought the two dwellings where Margie and Fred had been. They have transformed the place, with the help of their daughter Louise and son-in-law Julian. Sheila has made a wonderful garden and Jack has a pleasing kitchen garden. Both have devoted much time to Arthur, who tragically died early in the year 2000.

## Manger Cottage

This has been transformed from one of the original barns of Dennys Farm into a self-contained cottage. The current occupant is Jackie Foulds, who edits medical journals, mainly for the BMJ.

## Hill House *(formerly known as Dennys Farm, then Hill Farm, then The Pines)*

Somewhere in the archives of the Craddock family are some fifty documents dating back to 1666 relating to this property. It appears that many of the land deals were separate from deals to do with the farmhouse. Within the last one hundred and sixty years or so, the history of the place can be mapped in thus:

According to the Tithe records of 1839, George Calver (an ancestor of Ray Calver) owned just over seventy-three acres of what was then known as Dennys Farm, and John Mayhew managed it. In September 1846, Calver conveyed everything to John Crabtree. In 1851, roughly twenty acres were acquired from the Reverend John Holmes (who had owned two Wissett fields on the Rumburgh border) and Robert Tacon (one of the big land owners). From later maps, it can be seen that the three plots gained by Crabtree were Sheep's Hill and Great Pound Piece (that lie between the farm and Lodge Lane), and Bodkin's Hole, the narrow strip to the east of Stone Cottage, with the road on its north and the Beck running through it, opening out into a pond.

In 1871, Mary and Fanny Crabtree, who had inherited from their brother John Crabtree, conveyed the property to John Henry Gostling, 'Pharmaceutical Chymist' of Halesworth. This Mr Gostling died on 11 January 1906, and willed all his property, with the exception of his premises in the Market Place, Halesworth, to be auctioned off and the proceeds to be divided between his two sons.

So on 3 July 1906, Dennys Farm was duly auctioned to the highest bidder, Henry Edwin Garrod of Diss, for £1137 10s. This sum included the main farm buildings and about ninety-four acres of arable and pasture lands, and also the little cottage 'situate by the side of the private road now in occupation of Edward Cutts.' There are people today who can remember not only Mr Cutts, but his wife's parents, James and Martha Thurlow, who worked at the farm too. In the 1906 deed of conveyance, a William Squires is mentioned as having 'tenure' of the land from Gostling. Garrod bought the property free from encumbrances, bar a 'free rent payable to the Manor of Blythburgh late Priory of eight shillings' annually. Nobody seems to have bothered about paying this, as becomes evident later on.

Mr Garrod had the farm for only three years before joining with the financier Frederick Josiah Hucklesby of Stamford Hill, London, and arranging a sale to Charles Craddock of Bognor for £1175, of which Hucklesby got £100. A little map and memo attached to this 1909 sale document show that the small wedge of land south of the other Hill House (Lizzie Eagle Bott's cottage), to the east of the footpath on Great Pound Piece, was not sold to Mr Craddock but to a Mr Barber. The other item not sold to Craddock was 'the cottage' (which appears to signify Rose Cottage).

*James and Martha Thurlow,
who worked for the Gostlings
at Hill House (Dennys Farm)
in the late 1800s.*

The Craddocks remained at the farm until 1936. Many a Craddock tale diffused round the village. The most electrifying one concerned the fireball that squalled down the chimney into the parlour where Mr Craddock senior was dozing. It zoomed twice round the room and out through the window, which fortunately was open. The moral, Mr Craddock supposedly said, was always to keep a window open in a thunderstorm.

Charlie Craddock junior lived in the cottage by the driveway with his wife Eva (one of the four 'E's - daughters of Dick Baker of Stud Bungalow, the rest being Enid, Edna and Elsie). Charlie and Eva's four children had a big rocking-horse, which the farmworkers' children were allowed to play on, when they were invited in for a mug of Glaxo (a glucose drink).

In March 1936 Charles Craddock senior died, having appointed his wife and two sons executors and trustees. Stuart, the younger son, had moved to Devon so had no sentimental attachment to the farm, but Charlie, the older son, had remained in Wissett all the time, farming with his parents. Apparently he could not accept the majority decision

93

*The Pines' 1966*

to sell, and allowed his cows to trample over the tennis court in front of the house just before the new owners moved in during October 1938.

The newcomers were innovators. Mr and Mrs Richardson from Orford were determined to farm in a new and financially rewarding way. Mr Charles Richard Sugden Richardson, from the Indian Service of Engineers, was the first farmer in Wissett to start crop-spraying, and with Mr Lewis Rowe of Valley Farm, the first to introduce electricity into the village. Percy Davey, who worked for the Richardsons, was invited with his wife to the farm to watch television long before anyone else had a set.

At the outset, the Richardsons needed an income and local expertise. An early transaction was to let out half the farm for one year for a rent of £35 5s (from December 1938 - December 1939) to James Samuel Balls of High House Farm. The tenancy allowed Mr Balls the use of pasturage mainly, with some arable, plus most of the farm buildings except the 'donkey room.'

Mr Richardson then engaged himself in apple growing; and under the Lands Improvement Company's Scheme, obtained a loan for £565 to cover the cost of planting

94

27¹/₄ acres with dessert apples. With three other farms at Holton, Chediston and Peasenhall, Mr Richardson set up the WAGS (Waveney Apple Growers Scheme).

Residents today remember the apple orchards and the strawberry fields around them with various other plantations. Mrs Doreen Reeder (née Foster) recalls helping Mrs Alice Richardson milk her Jerseys as vividly as she remembers the tiger-skins that decorated the interior of the farmhouse.

Mr Richardson was by all accounts a canny businessman. He even drew up, on 24 June 1942, an official agreement with Mrs Grace Goldspink Goldspink (sic) of Wissett Grange opposite to grant her sewerage rights. For the privilege of letting her drain the 'discharge of the effluent' from her pipes that went under the road into his Bodkin's Hole (once a pond, now a disused pit) he quoted a yearly rental of one shilling.

By 1945 the Richardsons had bought the two houses in Wissett Street, Jubilee and Sunnyside, for their farmhands, and they had various wartime evacuees and workers lodging with them, amongst whom were Margaret Tamura, Ernest and Florence Scott, and Frederick Clements. During 1953 or 54 Charles Richardson bought Manor Farm for £3400, from Ian Dods (the personal representative of the Lewis Sanders Rowe estate) and Donald Meen, the occupant. Manor Farm at the time extended to about eighty-five acres, and included drovers' rights of way over a packway and driftway. Richardson then created Manor Farm (Wissett) Limited, and in 1956 he conveyed the whole of Manor Farm except for one field on The Pines side of the road into this company. At the same time, he conveyed his house Sunnyside into his company, plus his three fields: Lower Coles, Hobbles and Upper Coles which lay to the west of Box Farm.

Then in 1960, Richardson sold his field below the school to the council, and in 1964 he sold Jubilee House to Mrs Holden. He died in 1966, and his widow Alice sold up in 1968.

The next couple to take the farm on as a going concern were Mr and Mrs Brereton. They worked hard for four years before they moved. Eventually, Group Captain Lloyd Joel and his wife Mary bought the property, and with their vision, dedication and sheer hard work, they revitalized the whole estate, taking more than twenty-five years to do so. Lloyd was able to realize his life's dream of running a small beef cattle enterprise. When, in the course of time, Lloyd became very ill, the Joels had to take the hard decision to move to Aldeburgh. However, Mary Joel, having devoted herself to serving Lloyd through his fatal illness, has now taken up a new calling, as the Reverend Mary Joel in our Team ministry. The farmhouse has been happily sold to Camilla and Jeremy Prior, and much of the land to Andrew Howlett.

Camilla writes: 'When Jeremy and I came to look at The Pines with the children for the first time we knew immediately that it would make a perfect family house for us and none of us could quite believe the day we moved in. It was just before Christmas 1997, and the first thing we did was to introduce ourselves to Turvy, the Joels' cat, who they felt was too elderly to move. Oliver (born 1991), Howard(b 93), William(b 95) and Fudge our dog adored Turvy, particularly Fudge!' What the Priors particularly appreciate are the gardens, created by the Joels and their gardener Jerry Barber; the paddocks for their horses - thanks to the hard work of Andrew Howlett and his father John; the henhouse in the stable for Camilla's Black Rock hens; the chestnut trees, apples, blackberries, fishponds and wild birds.

## Manor Farm

In the 1830s and 40s according to the Tithe map, Manor Farm was part of Henry Bence Bence's big estate, which included Wissett Grange Farm and Pear Tree Farm. Bence was Lord of Thorington Manor, and exempt from paying tithes in Wissett. The loyalty of his farmworkers, who served Bence for up to sixty years, has already been commented on. In those days The Grange covered about sixteen and a quarter acres and Manor Farm eighty-five, sandwiching Box Farm, some of George Calver's fields, and Thomas Garrod's Mill Mount between its ploughlands.

By the turn of the century, the Bence estates in Wissett had all changed hands: in 1929, Stephen Hercules de Salis was handling Manor Farm. By 1933, it appears that Edward Donald Keen was running the place. Then the unforgettable Lewis Sanders Rowe, owner of Valley Farm, took on Manor Farm as well. George Sayer and family worked for Rowe and lived at Manor Farm until one of the Sayer daughters, Mabel, married Jo Kent (half-brother to Madge Cutts' first husband Herbert) who owned land at Westhall as well as Bonners Farm. George Sayer went to work for Jo Kent, vacating Manor Farm to Donald Meen, who had already been working with his father Jimmy for Rowe at Valley Farm.

Lewis Rowe died on 10 December 1951 and his estate fell to Edith Marion Rowe. She in turn died on 16 March 1954, having appointed Ian Walter Dods (in Dorset) as trustee. Dods and Meen made a legal transaction, whereby they sold Manor Farm to CRS Richardson of The Pines. Richardson consequently created his company, Manor Farm (Wissett) Limited.

After Charles Richardson's death in 1966, Martin Kempe, who had already been WAGS advisor to Richardson, bought the farmhouse and half the land. He had been a horticultural consultant in Lowestoft and Aldeby (where the dryers for the apples were) and he had spent a year in Africa as a volunteer horticulturist on an Oxfam market gardening project in the Sahel region. He undertook a considerable restoration programme for Manor Farm. During the latter years of Richardson's time, the building had been used as an apple-storage barn, not as a house at all. Mr Kempe preserved a wall of lath and plaster that had survived (just) from late mediaeval times, and restored the main hall with its magnificent chestnut wood beams. Many local people worked for Martin picking apples, and there were always students during the holidays who received board and lodging as well. Peter Cutts worked for Martin along with Kevin Nunn, Sugar Nunn's grandson, from 1983 to 97. Martin's friend Peter Kelly came from London every year to help with the picking as well. Kevin Nunn remembers those times of huge community spirit, when pickers from all over the countryside would gather at Manor Farm for the harvest.

After a good ten years, however, with ever more stringent competition from foreign markets, and supermarkets increasingly setting the price rather than the shareholders of the WAGS consortium, Martin Kempe retired and moved to Norwich in 1997.

The present owners of the house are Patrick Newton, formerly the proprietor of the Halesworth chemist's shop, and Lesley Jones who works for her brother in Yoxford at a fine arts press, and who has designed layouts for the local community newsletter, *The Wissett Web*. Lesley is, moreover, acclaimed as a fly-fishing champion. There are four children: Freddie, Katie, Max and Ralph. The house is at present undergoing major improvements. The land has been further divided; few apple orchards remain. 'Tough measures' from Europe have forced change to the landscape of Manor Farm no less than to fruit-farms everywhere in the county.


## Manor Farm Cottage

Some of Manor Farm land was bought by Ian and Nicola Timmins along with the holiday home that Martin Kempe had converted from the old stables. A tree had fallen on the building during the gales in 1987 and all but demolished it. Manor Farm Cottage was constructed from the remains. Ian and Nicky have kept what orchards they bought, and use the apples to make juice. They have some fifty Gloucestershire Old Spot pigs, about thirty sheep and two alpacas all reared organically. Ian is a birds of prey enthusiast and keeps a goshawk and a cooperhawk, while Nicky enjoys horseriding. She is a nursery teacher at Ilketshall St Lawrence School. The Timmins sons are Mark and Gary.


## Box Farm

This appears to have been a mediaeval box-framed house, similar to Tudor Cottage. However, it has been so neatly renovated in the last ten years that it is difficult to be precise.

In the 1830s it was farmed by James Ecclestone and owned by Guiseppa Wright, who was married to Jonathan Marchant Esquire, a landowner outside the area. Box Farm was a modest smallholding of some twenty-eight acres of arable and pastureland. The 1881 directories show that the running of the farm had passed to George Jordan (grandfather of John Jordan, and also of Phyllis Flaxman, née Jordan). He remained here with his wife Ann (Maria), eight children and a number of in-laws for many years. One of his daughters, Elsie, married Henry Halifax, whose father owned Nos 9 and 10 The Street during World War I. By 1922, Jordan had Edward Elderkin working under him, and the Elderkin family living at the farm, while George and John Jordan are listed as farming at Rumburgh as well. Mrs Ada Annie Elderkin (1854-1938) devoted herself to her invalid husband Edward - who by many accounts never left his bed - and to her two sons, Jo and Harry, who were christened by the schoolchildren Mr Day and Mr Night. Ironically, Mr Edward Elderkin outlived his wife by a year, and since his other children had left home, he had to be cared for by the two sons who were themselves in need of care. Jo, Mr Day, would only venture out in daylight and was not strong; Harry, Mr Night, 'suffered from nerves,' say eye-witnesses, and would only be seen at night, quietly pedalling his bike. Elizabeth Davey still has a silver thimble given to her as a girl by Mrs Elderkin in the 1930s, when Elizabeth and her grandmother, Nellie Oxborough, would go up to Box Farm every Friday for a pound of Mrs Elderkin's butter.

After everyone at Box Farm had died except Harry, Lloyd Joel, who had come with his family to live at The Pines opposite in 1972, was a frequent visitor to Harry, who was quite paranoid about leaving the house at all. Lloyd spent many hours a week comforting and chatting to him. Eventually, when Harry was gone, the property fell to the descendants of the other children. It is now, after complete restoration, let out to Paul Reason, a former pilot. An interesting discovery Paul has made among the books lying in the old parlour is an almanac stating that the curates of Wissett lived here at Box Farm for centuries, not, as one might think, at the parsonage next to the church. The truth of the almanac is not proven.

*George, Freddie, Johnny, Rachel, Minnie and Lily (mother of Ray Beales): six Nunns of Hill Farm.*

## Hill Farm

Hill Farm dates from roughly 1540 and is thought to have been called Gull Farm at one time ('gull' referring to a stream or beck). Kevin Nunn believes that there was a previous dwelling on the spot back in the thirteenth century. The 1840 Tithe return shows that Thomas Self owned and worked what was a smallholding of seven acres then. He was there until the mid 1860s, and was succeeded by a Mr John March. In 1874 a Mr Tuffs bought the place for his seven-year-old daughter, Sarah. The 1881 census lists John March, now aged seventy, as a machine-owner and farmer still at the farm with his wife Maria and a two-year-old grandson, Walter March. Whether he managed the farm for Sarah Tuffs is only guesswork, but he was presumably allowed to retire there, while George Nunn was starting to farm at Hill Farm in the early 1890s. George Nunn married Sarah Tuffs and acceded to Hill Farm. George, himself one of ten children, went on with

Sarah to have ten children, of whom some - for instance, James, Minnie and William - figure elsewhere. Of the rest, Rachel married Mr Watker and died only a couple of years ago aged over 103; Annie married Jimmy Coman; Lizzie married Mr Head and lived in Fressingfield; George 'The Banker' (because he was so careful with money) worked the post office in Rumburgh; Lily married Alec Beales who worked at Manor Farm with another Nunn brother, Freddie. Johnny was the brother who stayed at Hill Farm working with his father. Johnny describes the extraordinary layout of the house. The stairs got progressively deeper in their treads the higher you climbed. As you headed for the attics, Johnny and his family used to joke that you needed one leg three inches longer than the other.

The great George Nunn was known as 'Sugar Nunn.' Ingenious reasons are provided for this accolade: it was because his forefathers had worked in the treacle pits (in the hemp industry); or, because George used to give sweets to children; or, it was to sweeten his famous temper. The nickname remained and was inherited by all the Nunn children. George used to go about in his horse-drawn cart selling a variety of produce such as chickens, plums, peanuts and fish. The local blacksmith in Rumburgh, Allen Clarke, remembers having to strengthen the cart-springs on the side where George sat. George died in 1937 but the farm stayed in the family with Johnny taking it on. During the war, Johnny spent some time at Melton Mowbray looking after prisoners of war and working with them, in gangs, in agriculture. Johnny's son Kevin worked over the way at Manor Farm, and his daughter Margaret (Jean) married Robin Baxter and moved from the village. Johnny grew corn and kept some cattle and pigs. Johnny's wife suffered dreadfully from cancer, so after much debate, in 1981, the family moved to Halesworth, relinquishing their much-loved farm to Shirley Wickman, who is still there today. She keeps three Red Polls, a horse and some geese and a couple of dogs. Meanwhile, Johnny and Kevin still visit Wissett regularly, and are often seen quietly honouring their family graves in the churchyard.

*James Nunn working at Hill Farm before the First World War.*

*Lewis Rowe of Valley Farm*

## Valley Farm

This is another of the early farmsteads, probably over four hundred years old. By the mid 1800s it was owned by William Dearn Calver and farmed by George Calver junior, Hector and Roger's grandfather. Towards the end of the century it passed to John Whitehead (or Whitehand) and then to William Harry Brothers. By 1912 Sidney Lampshire was farming there, and then Charles Manuelle in 1925. The next owner was Henry Raymond Gorst, the man who accidentally ran over Kenny Debenham who came rushing out into the road, straight into Mr Gorst's open-top racing car. People say that he never got over the shock, and died young - only thirty - although he actually died of appendicitis in 1932. His gaunt headstone stands in the south east corner of the churchyard: a huge cross.

Lewis Rowe, the next owner of Valley Farm, came from Oulton Broad with his sister Edith. In spite of his fabled drinking bouts, he did much for the village. Those who remember him look quite desolate when they describe his lonely death in 1951, and the auction of his silver and furniture, which each took a whole day to sell off. Pinto Reeder fondly recalls the days that he worked for Rowe. For three years running Pinto won the Ploughing Cup (1938, 39 and 40) at the Drawing Matches that Rowe would organize at Valley Farm. Jo Aldridge, whose parents ran The Swan, devoted his youth from the age of fourteen working for Mr Rowe, who eventually became a diabetic and relied on Jo to help him inject insulin every morning.

After Lewis and Edith were gone, Edward de las Casas bought Valley Farm in about 1954. He and his wife Deirdre brought up their children there. Hugh, their son, married Alice Colby, whose parents Dick and Mary lived at Millcroft, up Mill Road. After the family had grown up, they sold in 1970 to Anne and Robert Myhill from Rumburgh. There were fifteen acres of land all told, but when Anne and Robert left in 1976 they retained ten acres, and sold the house with five acres to Anne and Michael Antram, who came from Brighton with Granny Antram, aged about ninety. They were artists and very enthusiastic about country crafts. They lowered the floor of the farmhouse and re-laid original pammets.

The present owners are Janet and Jonathan Craft. They moved here from Buckinghamshire in about 1986. Jonathan, a civil engineer, pursued his dream to set up a vineyard and bought two thousand vines from Alsace. They used as their label a detail from one of the bosses high in the roof of Norwich cathedral: Noah tending his vines. The first vintage produced 845 bottles. Unfortunately Jonathan's work took him overseas, so while the house is rented out the vines are not producing wine at the moment.

## Rumburghplace Farm

This farmstead has been associated for many centuries with pottery making. Local archaeological records pinpoint the Sterff family, who originated in Weybread in the late Middle Ages, as having kilns not only in Metfield and Chediston but also in Wissett, probably on this site. The present owner of the farmhouse, Mrs Angela Armour-Chelu, has written for *The Wissett Web* a fascinating account of the discovery in 1972 of early sixteenth century German stoneware and locally-made pottery, horseshoes, bridle pieces, spurs, pilgrims' badges, Nuremburg traders' tokens and other finds.

Evidence of links with the pottery and the hemp industries remain in the field names: Potter's Hill, Retting Pit Close and Retting Pit Piece.

In the 1830s, Robert Chase owned and farmed a good sixty acres here. From the 1850s, the farm was known as Moores Farm and run by the Moore family for several generations. The 1881 census lists Robert Moore as a widower of forty-nine, and five children: Arthur, the oldest at twenty-five, followed by Elizabeth, Robert, Thomas and Alice, the youngest at eight.

William Hadingham took over the farm in 1914, and, followed by his two sons, Stanley and Wilfred, farmed Rumburghplace until 1968, when it was divided and sold.

Wilfred, who had been residing at the farmhouse, went to Reydon; Stanley and his wife had already been living since 1953 up the road in 'Westlyn,' the bungalow built on a small plot of their farmland.

In 1969, Ian and Angela Armour-Chelu, both artists, moved from Westleton to the farm, where they raised their four daughters. Ian died in 2000 and is greatly missed.

Angela Armour-Chelu writes: 'Rumburghplace Farm is set on the edge of the old Rumburgh with Wissett Common, and when we first came here in 1969 the area was particularly beautiful. The farmland had already been sold off from the farmhouse, but there were still the ancient meadows with ponds, hedges and great elm trees. Now it is just one great field, with either winter wheat or oil seed rape. To the right of the house towards Rumburgh there were the remains of a deserted village or settlement and in the evening when the sun was low we could see the pattern of houses and sunken streets. Red House Farm, diagonally opposite to us, was still standing then, and the back wing of Hill Farm (opposite us towards Linstead) had still not been rebuilt. The bungalow at the top of our drive wasn't there either. A number of the farms had small dairy herds and would set out maybe one or two churns of milk at the ends of their drives to be collected in the morning. There were skylarks in the sky and kingfishers by the ponds. In winter the fields were full of lapwings. And in the early autumn we could count up to fifty swallows ready to depart - we haven't had swallows or martins here now for the last five years.'

*Rumburghplace Farm*

# Moors Lodge

At the top of Sugar Nunn's Hill, lies this large bungalow built on a field formerly called Barn Pightle next to the barns of Rumburghplace Farm by Christabel and Wilfred Flatt in about 1973, when they moved from Ash Farm in the nearby village of All Saints. The Flatts farmed several acres of land adjacent to the bungalow until they retired in 1990 or so, moving to Harleston. Their son John, who remained at Ash Farm, still farms the land.

Jeananne and William Rennie Smith, who arrived from Geldermalsen in the Netherlands, bought this bungalow in August 1993. Jeananne, who trained as a dental nurse, was an instructor in the Red Cross, and belonged to the Voluntary Aid Detachment. She worked in the Royal Infirmary, Liverpool, the City Hospital, Derby, and the Derbyshire Royal Infirmary on the wards. Rennie, after an Exhibition to Cambridge, did his National Service with the Royal Engineers. From 1970, he became first a member, then a fellow, of the Institution of Electrical Engineers. Having risen to head of the Electrification Section of British Railways Research Division, Rennie was then seconded to the Research Office of the International Union of Railways in the Netherlands. He retired as deputy director in 1993.

While still travelling widely, the couple have become stalwarts of the village, involved in church fund-raising, clerical and financial services to the PCC (of which Rennie was treasurer for some years).

The Smiths are devoted grandparents, keen opera-goers, and seasoned sailors.

# Westlyn

For more than thiry-five years, this was the home of Mr and Mrs Stanley Hadingham. Stanley's parents had returned to the area from Woodbridge in 1914 with their two young sons. They had settled in Rumburghplace Farm, and Stanley and his brother Wilfred had attended school in Wissett, but Rumburgh Sunday School. It was here that Stanley met his wife, Ivy, the daughter of Freddie Woods who was bailiff to members of the Lawn family first in Rumburgh then at Wissett Place. They married in 1925, spent six years at South Elmham All Saints, twenty-one years in Rumburgh, and then moved into Westlyn, which was newly-built for them in 1953.

Whilst farming at Rumburghplace Farm, Ivy and Stanley gave many years of service to the local community. Stanley was clerk to Rumburgh Parish Council for forty-three years, a member of Rumburgh Parochial Church Council for almost as long, and churchwarden for thirty-three years. Ivy, who had been only sixteen when she was appointed church organist, carried on playing the organ for more than sixty years. Their only child, Vera, who became sister-in-law to Freda Kerrison, sadly predeceased them.

Now Westlyn is home not only to Donald and Hilda Bloss, but seven ewes, one ram, and seven goats on two acres of land. Having retired from Leiston in October 1988, the Blosses bought Westlyn after the death of Ivy Hadingham in March 1989.

## Byebrue Kennels

Walter and Kate Thompson built this bungalow in the 1950s and set up a pig breeding unit with a pedigree herd of Landrace pigs. The premises were then called Thornfields and comprised some three acres of land. Subsequently, a Mr and Mrs Addison owned the piggeries for a few years before handing over to Mr and Mrs Hayes from Somerset (via Wenhaston). The Hayes persevered with pig breeding for as long as possible. Inevitably, the time came when to continue with the pigs proved uneconomical, so the stock was sold. At the same time, Eileen Hayes was breeding Great Dane dogs. There was a need for boarding kennels in the area so most of the pig units were demolished and rebuilt as kennels. The name 'Byebrue' derives from the River Brue in Somerset, near the Hayes' home for nineteen years before their transition to Suffolk.

Mr Robin Westward and Mr Ralph Windle bought the refurbished kennels next, but were only here for a couple of years before selling to Daphne and Terry Bourne. Less than three further years elapsed before the Bournes moved on as well. Helen and Paul Hunter, from Wheathampstead in Hertfordshire, have been the new owners since December 1999. They have continued with the Boarding Kennels and Cattery and in addition provide an animal grooming service.

## Hors Farm

Susa and Bruce Crompton, with their children Lois and Max and several dogs, live in this lovely old thatched house. They came from Essex in 1990 and have undertaken a number of repairs and improvements. James Ball rethatched the roof for them in 1994-5.

The farmstead dates from approximately 1427, although little is known of its owners until the Tithe record of 1839-41, which lists William Pattison Esq as proprietor and William Banks as farming about forty acres for him. The 1844 White's Directory shows William Banks as owner of Hawes Farm (as it was then called), and followed by James Banks, probably a son, right through until the turn of the century. According to the 1881 census, James was sixty-seven, and farming sixty acres by then, with his wife Mary Ann, who was fifty-five. Living in the farmhouse with them was one servant, Charles Butcher, aged sixteen. It appears that nearby on the estate was another household of servants: the Page family. The parents, George and Patricia, were in their thirties, while their four children, Margaret, Alice, Fred and Sidney were all under ten.

Mary Ann Banks remained until at least 1908, helped out from about 1900 by Benjamin Reeder. By 1916, Horace Lawn was running 'Hawes,' while Benjamin was farming at the now demolished Red House Farm on Rumburgh Common. By 1922, his son Leonard Reeder was working at both Pear Tree Farm, Rumburgh, and at Red House Farm to help his father, whose back had grown very bent. Shortly afterwards, Benjamin, Leonard and his wife Harriet and their two little girls, Cathy and Dorothy, moved to Hors Farm, as it then became known. Pinto Reeder, Leonard and Harriet's third child, was born there, followed by his sister Olive, before the family relocated to Hill House Farm up the road.

It would appear that the Banks' descendants owned the property well into the 1920s, with Leonard Reeder farming for them until at least 1925. By 1929 John Edward Hambling and his wife Ethel Helen were the owners. During the Second World War, they had a German prisoner of war working for them, known as Henry Williams. After the war was over, Henry decided to stay and he lived with and worked for the Hamblings, immersing himself in village life. He is buried in Wissett churchyard. Ethel Hambling is remembered for her homemade wine and the numerous chickens she kept. When a visitor arrived, she would sweep the chickens off the kitchen table and offer a glass of her potato or wheat wine. The visitors would remember arriving but seldom how they got home! The Hamblings' son Basil and his wife Lily lived with them for several years before moving to 13 Brickhill Cottages. After Ethel died, her husband John moved to Mells and sold the farm to a group of people who ran an organic market garden, which included growing cereals and specialist research crops for the Henry Doubleday Research Association. The next owners of the farm were Theodore Scott and partner, who were theatrical costumiers. They restored the farm lovingly, over a period of some eight years, before selling to Susa and Bruce Crompton. The farm became Hors Farm again, reverting to its roots in the mediaeval Rogere le Hore, who in 1327 had to pay a Subsidy Return of XXd, or twenty pence.

*Hors Farm 1972*

## Tarleton *(formerly Little Hill Farm)*

Trudy and Richard (Rick) Ceculski live in this charming seventeenth-century thatched cottage, having come from Peasenhall, along with several horses, in 1992. It was they who changed the name to Tarleton, after a much-loved horse that had died. They have extended the cottage, and carried out major restorations

Tarleton's past history is sketchy. From the 1839-41 Tithe returns, one can see that John Fiske farmed here and at Sildan House one hundred and fifty acres for George Parkyns of Chediston Hall. The 1881 census reveals a shepherd, Horace Hamstling, living here or close by, with his wife Eliza and daughter Laura. It is plausible that the John Hambling who lived here at the turn of the century was a relation, since experience of the old directories demonstrates that spellings were often unstable, and that names could undergo a completely unrecognizable transformation within a generation! Notwithstanding John Hambling's genealogy, he stayed at Tarleton long enough for his wife Emily to give birth to their son Freddie. John was horseman to Mr Banks at Hawes Farm.

Dolly (née Newsome) and Robert (Rocky) Spall were among the most hardy characters to inhabit this smallholding. There were about twenty-five acres all told, which Rocky kept as arable, with no grazing for his six or seven head of cattle. So every evening at about 7 pm, he would set off with the cattle and feed them on the road verges, walking in front of them, closing any open gates that they might get through. He would travel as far as Walpole some evenings, not returning until midnight. This was apparently commonplace among small farmers then. Rocky would go to Beccles Sale every Friday with his horse and cart; Dolly would see him out of the gate and would be there to open it when he came home. She apparently never went out.

Mr and Mrs Jimmy Meen and their family lived here briefly after moving from Sildan house and before they moved into Wissett Street in 1931, but who the next residents were is not remembered.

Two elderly ladies were stationed here during the war, with spy-thriller names: Miss Dorothy McTurk and Miss Van Heuten.

# Hill House Farm

We are not sure of the year that this old farmhouse was founded but the 1841 Tithe record states that it was owned by Nathaniel Micklethwaite and occupied by James Carley, as a farm of seventy-four acres then. From the 1881 census, it is evident that two well-known families had branches farming here: Reeders and Seamans. Henry Reeder (Benjamin's brother) is listed as managing eighty-seven acres and employing two men. He was forty at the time, while his wife, Lucy, was considerably older. The two men employed appear to be John Seamans and his son Frederick, who, although only fourteen, is detailed as 'agricultural labourer.' The Seamans lived on site or nearby; as well as father and oldest son, were Eliza, John's wife, and four more children under twelve: Charles, David, Arthur, and the baby Christina.

At the end of the 1800s, the farm was owned by a group of people: Reverend Cecil Mills, John Digby Mills, James Herbert Benyon, Francis Gustavus Nicholls and Robert Edmund Ford. In 1901 it was in the ownership of Messrs Francis Horner & Son of Norwich and still rented to Henry Reeder. Some time afterwards, William Hurren took on the running of the farm, but in 1912 he and the family moved to Halesworth and started Hurren's butchers shop, which is today run by William's grandson, Dick Hurren.

The fortunes of the farm at the beginning of the First World War are uncertain, but Edward Guy Godbold is listed in the Kelly's directories as running it from at least 1916 until the mid 1920s, when he settled at Whitehouse Farm. His protégé, Pilfer Chapman, then moved up here from Halleluia. By 1929 Leonard Reeder (Henry's nephew) had brought his family, including his father, Benjamin, here from Hors Farm.

Leonard used to get his oldest daughter, Cathy, and his oldest son, Pinto, to milk the cows with him before they went to school. Pinto recounts the tragi-comic demise of his grandfather Benjamin. It was a dark, stormy night in December 1929. Benjamin, who walked with two sticks, was negotiating the little bridge over a ditch by the path, on his return from visiting a neighbour. One of his granddaughters flashed a light onto the bridge to show Benjamin where to tread. Unfortunately he missed his footing and fell into the freezing water. Sid Gardiner, living nearby, heard the cries and hurried over. As a naval man he was skilled in first aid. He carried Benjamin indoors and pumped the water out of his lungs. Benjamin groaned and moaned all night, to such an extent that everyone thought he was getting better. Ironically, he was not, and died from shock and cold.

Leonard's younger son John recalls when the ammunition dump at Metfield barn exploded during the war and all the thatch in the barn roof came down on top of him. John was one of the second 'batch' of the eight children. Cathy, Dorothy, Harold and Olive had been born before the move to Hill House Farm, where the rest were born: Edna, John, Edwin and Alan. After leaving school at fifteen, John worked for his father on the farm.They used to grow sugar beet, wheat, barley, beans and cattle beet. Leonard and the family rented the farm until 1956 when it was bought, from the Norwich business, by John and Jill Howlett, who arrived from Bruisyard with their son Andrew and daughter Maryanne. Leonard and Harriet Reeder moved into St Peter's Farmhouse, Wissett, and John and his wife Mary moved to Spexhall. John continued working at the farm for John Howlett, until he retired in 1998.

The Howletts are still farming Hill House Farm but their son Andrew has taken over the day to day running of it. In 1983 John and Jill had an extension built onto the farmhouse and they moved into it, (calling it Hill Farm, to the consternation of the postman!) leaving Andrew, his wife Mairi and their three children: James, William and Juliette in the original farmhouse.

John will be remembered for the long hours and effort he put into the organizing and running of the Wissett Treacle Fairs. He and Jill are still very involved with the village, and are members of Wissett Bowls Club, but now that they are semi-retired, they enjoy travelling.

## Sildan House *(formerly Halls Cottages)*

The 1841 Tithe map indicates a homestead here along with several acres of land. It was owned by George Parkyns and farmed by John Fiske. This dwelling was probably demolished to build the present house in around 1900. It was built, possibly for farmworkers, as a double tenement. The first known residents were Mr and Mrs Jimmy Meen who inhabited the end furthest from the road, with Billy Hambling next door. This was in 1924, when the Meens came from Linstead. Roly Meen remembers being here when he was about four, and his mother had lots of chickens and rabbits. They moved down the road to Tarleton (Little Hill Farm then), while Ted and Emily Pretty moved in with their son John. Next door, after Billy Hambling, were Sam and 'Ducky' Hunting with their son Charlie. Both Ted and Sam worked in Chediston for Mr Ingate who no doubt owned the cottages then. Ducky is remembered as an exceptionally diligent worker who would labour out in the fields during harvest and then go thrashing with her husband! She is, moreover, renowned for her highly colourful vocabulary.

Mrs Ivy Connor, the present owner, retired here from London in 1964 with her husband, who regrettably died in 1981. Ivy, a Yorkshire lass, had met her husband in London while they were both in the Forces during the war. Their three children all live in the London area.

## Church Cottage

At eye-level on the inside wall of the church tower is an old notice-board whose text refers to this cottage.
It reads:

> Property belonging to the Parish of Wissett
> Town House adjoining the Churchyard at the South
> west corner. held on lease, which was Granted by
> the Church-warden and overseer of the above Parish
> from the 5th. of July 1772 for 99 years at the Annual
> Ground Rent of £1.5.0. which sum has been always
> applied to the repairs of the Church. Lease expires
> on the 5th. of July 1873 and the House is now occupied
> by Samuel Jackson and Robert Cooper.
> > John Tillott
> > John Button  churchwardens 1846

This tallies more or less with White's Directory of 1844, although the first date should read 1774, and the rent, £1 5s 4d It is clear that the cottage had been 'vested in trust from an early period,' and was owned by 'Parish Officers.' It was divided into two dwellings.

The earliest person within living memory to have dwelt in the left-hand side was Shilly Mouser. People now in their seventies and eighties remember Shilly's only son

Freddie at school with them in the 1920s. To his embarrassment, Freddie nearly always had to wear a wide frilly collar to school. For a while, the Mousers had another boy lodging with them: Danny Lloyd. Shilly - officially Mr George Mouser, the roadsweep - told someone when he was a lad that he earned a 'shilly' a week. That name stayed with him always. He kept the banks and verges immaculate, from Wissett Hall at the Halesworth end, through Wissett village to Valley Farm driveway. With his extra-long bristled broom and shovel balanced across his cart, he was a familiar sight. He was very thin and turned his feet out with his hob-nailed boots on. After his wife's death, Shilly and Freddie moved to Brickhill Cottages with the housekeeper.

After the Mousers, Sugar Nunn's son Freddie moved in with his wife Lucy, who was the daughter of Puff Seaman at The Swan. Lucy died tragically of TB. In the other half of the cottages lived a Mrs Burroughs with her daughters Gladys and Lillian (who had a family connection to William Burroughs the village coal dealer in Victorian times). Children were sympathetic to Gladdie, who had a withered arm, but were curious about Lillian, who was officially Mrs Jarman, and 'washed' for the Walkers at Wissett Lodge. She had two daughters, Shirley and Brenda, and then a third, who was christened Mabel.

Arnold Read (Ernie) - who was a boy in the early 1900s, one of the sons of the shop-keepers at No 33 The Street - had been a shepherd in his youth at Halleluia Cottage. He subsequently moved with his wife Phyllis to Church Cottages, where he suffered not only with a withered arm (acquired, it is said, by gassing in the war) but also with the onset of lung cancer. His sorrowful death came in 1950, when he was only fifty-four. He and Phyllis (who died in 1986) share a memorial stone in the shape of an open book in Wissett churchyard.

The cottage changed hands in the 1950s, and was rented out as holiday lets. Robert and Margery Wetmore from London bought the cottage in 1963 for £800. Between lettings, they lived here 'on and off for around twenty years,' as Lizzie Eagle Bott writes in her memoirs. 'Then tragedy struck and after a long illness, Margery died from cancer. I was devastated. Robert had died two years earlier. It was a terrible blow to have lost them both.'

Church Cottage was then bought by Bill Parks who lives in the cottage now. Robert and Margery Wetmore had already put in years of labour doing the basic groundwork (before their time, the cottage had only one outside tap).

Mary Kirk arrived in the village just before Christmas 1997, fell in love with the cottage and rented it from Bill until February 2000. Mary is an artist, and the discerning author of such books as *Holy Matrimony? An Exploration of Ministry and Marriage.* She is committed to village activities, particularly organizing the Wissett Art Show and church fund-raising. For one event, she is known to have cycled round forty churches in one day. Since Bill Parks and his family have returned to their cottage, Mary has moved temporarily to Spexhall, from which vantage point she still participates in Wissett life.

*Rose Cottage*

## Rose Cottage

In the nineteenth century, this cottage was owned by Thomas Self (who also owned Hill Farm) and occupied by Thomas Briggs. A century later, Doreen Foster (now Mrs Reeder) lived there as a girl with her parents before moving to No 7 The Street.

Two Nunn brothers lived in this cottage with their families, although not all at once! James and Helen Nunn were here with their daughter Joyce, until about 1926, when they moved to one of the cottages on the Wissett Hall estate. Willie Nunn and his wife Alice with their two rosy daughters were here briefly before transferring to another of the cottages attached to Wissett Hall, where Willie was kicked by one of the Red Poll cows and had to have his leg amputated.

Another couple who stayed at Rose Cottage before the Second World War was William (Uncle Winter) and Mary Oxborough, with their daughter Hilda. At the end of the war, a Mr and Mrs Wiggins were evacuated here. 'They were true cockneys,' remembers one of the ladies who was born and bred in Wissett, ' but they enjoyed Wissett so much that they stayed on. Mrs Wiggins had a navy-blue dress with white polka-dots on, and her husband Bill used to say he couldn't resist her when she was wearing it: "Poor old Bill, he'd die on the nest!" Hector Calver told Annie Oxborough.' Miss Lizzie Eagle Bott used to take the Wiggins water in buckets, until with the passage of time they grew frail. Mrs Wiggins died and her husband went into care, to drive in his imagination the engines that he had driven in reality for so many years in London. Lizzie bought Rose Cottage, fumigated and renovated it. Dick Colby, who lived up Mill Road, built a summer-house onto the south wall. Lizzie's tenants included a welfare officer, a woman police officer ('Busty Bertha'), then a Dr and Mrs White, whose son married PD James, who at that time worked in the Home Office. Dr White's family loved Rose Cottage, and PD James wrote her first crime novel, *Cover Her Face*, partly there and partly in Lizzie's cottage next door. PD James' fictional detective, Inspector Dalgliesh, had an aunt, Jane Dalgliesh. This splendid creation owes much to the real-life Lizzie Eagle Bott. Such gems as,' to her individual, dégagé elegance was added the hint of a contemporary smartness,' and, 'She was sitting, as always, bolt upright and yet she looked perfectly comfortable. She was knitting a pair of woollen socks in bright red which Dalgliesh could only hope were not intended for him. He thought it unlikely. His aunt was not given to such tokens of affection. The firelight threw gules on her long face, brown and carved as an Aztec's, the eyes hooded, the nose long and straight above a wide mobile mouth,' are recognizably Lizzie, to whom, as to Jane Dalgliesh, 'people were as they were.'

The Whites vacated Rose Cottage after five years. Lizzie let it out to her cousin Harry Ritchie, who was becoming rather frail. After his death in Blythburgh Hospital, Arthur ('Whippy') Simpson from the Water Board came to Rose Cottage to retire and spend his happiest ten years as Lizzie's gardener, until his death in 1979. Eventually, Lizzie sold the cottage to Arthur's nephew Denis Simpson who is in the printing industry, and his wife Christine, a receptionist at Patrick Stead Hospital in Halesworth. Denis holds the key to the church tower, where from time to time he hoists commemorative flags, such as the Union Jack, for special occasions. Denis is a keen golfer and cricketer while Christine is a devoted gardener.

## Hill House

This house was built by William Haggar in the early 1800s; the present owners, Valerie and Peter Eagle-Bott, tell us that Haggar's initials 'WH' are fixed on the north side of the house. William's widow Susanna paid tithes in the 1830s and 40s, and is buried in the churchyard, by the path to Lodge Lane. She died in 1846, in her nineties.

For many years, the house was in the hands of two connected families: the Rogers and the Manns, whose uniform headstones and graves line the church path leading from the bridge. Jack, Laura and Harriet Mann are names that linger in wartime memories.

The most colourful owner of the house to bestride the post-war decades of the twentieth century was Miss Elizabeth Eagle Bott (Lizzie). As she writes in her memoirs:

'I found the cottage on a sunny May morning. I looked over the gate and saw a small house in need of considerable repair. It was completely surrounded by a very overgrown garden. On the far side there was an orchard full of fruit trees which were covered with blossom. Over the road from the orchard was a beautiful Norman church.'

She goes on to write that the cottage had once been divided into two, with two living rooms 'with little black cooking stoves, two pantries and two small washing rooms.' There was no water, not even a well, no lighting and only an outside privy.

Lizzie decided that she was going to live there, come what may, even though at the time the owner, Mrs Rogers, did not want to sell. Lizzie got her way, and employed Sid Johnson (one of the famed Johnson family who had built Nos 9 and 10 The Street, Wissett) to renovate the place, lay on electricity and flush lavatory. On 16 May 1947, Lizzie, helped by her cousin May, moved in. Lizzie remembers the age before the car, the age of the pony and trap, of Waxy Hard the cobbler at No 19 The Street, of Billy Thompson's father (the policeman who promoted sport in the village), of the two shops, and the two pubs.

On Rogation Sunday in 1973, Lizzie was a triumphant character atop a float, playing the harmonium. She played the organ in the church for many years and was tirelessly involved with village activities and fund-raising, right up to her death in the spring of 1999.

The cottage has passed to Lizzie's first cousin once removed, Peter Eagle-Bott, and his wife Valerie, who have worked ceaselessly to effect a magical transformation of both house and grounds. The couple have come up from Etchinghill in Kent, but they had been visiting Lizzie at Hill House for the last thirty years. Peter's great-grandmother had been a daughter of Thomas Wilson of Hull - founder of the Wilson Shipping Line. The Baccarat Case scandal took place at her brother's house: Tranby Croft, Hull.

# Lodge Cottages

Both cottages were built in about 1927-28 for farm workers at Lodge Farm.

## I Lodge Cottage

Grace and Fred Warren lived in No I with their sons: David, John and Roy, who all now live in bungalows on the Wissett Road, Halesworth. After the Warrens, Jim Ingate, who had married Millie Cutts, came with their little son Ronnie from a small cottage opposite Hill Farm up near Rumburgh. Their daughter Pearl was born at Lodge Cottage. When the war ended, they moved to Holton, and the Kiddy family arrived at The Lodge. Various people were here as tenants of the Kiddys, before the present owners, Carol Woanes and Don Watts, came in 1999 from Norwich. Both work for Adnams.

## 2 Lodge Cottage

Before the war, Dan Woolner and his family lived here. With the coming of the Kiddys, while Dorothy and Albert Kiddy lived at Wissett Lodge, their son Gerald and his wife Margaret lived in this cottage as newly-weds.

A generation later, when Gerald and Margaret were installed at The Lodge, their son Geoffrey and his new wife Claire (née Brinton) lived in this cottage until they in turn moved up to The Lodge. Gerald and Margaret retired to Wenhaston.

Tracey and Paul Wisdom arrived here in 1997 with their daughter, Megan, who is now seven. Tracey ( from Southwold) trained in classical music then extended her career into folk-singing. She regularly performs in folk clubs and pubs, and is well-known for her singing in Wissett church. Paul likewise is a musician. Outwardly he is in the freight and shipping business at Felixstowe; inwardly, Paul is really 'Wiz' the wizard pop singer and guitarist.

*Lady Ottoline Morrell who visited Wissett Lodge in 1916.*

113

## Wissett Lodge

The manorial history of The Lodge is exciting but complex. It has been well documented by the Wissett and District Local History Group, so only a fraction of its intricate records are touched on here.

From the time of *Domesday* in 1086, the site of Wissett Lodge has had connections with three manorial traditions:

1. Wissett Manor, which was linked to the names of Sir Robert de Ufford, Sir Robert de Swillington (who both held estates all over Suffolk in the fourteenth century) and John Hopton. Wissett Manor in John Hopton's day was absorbed by Wissett le Roos, the best known of the manors.

2. The turbulent history of Wissett/Wissett le Roos started well before the Conquest, and was documented in *Domesday* and the *Anglo-Saxon Chronicle* with the mention of Ralph the Staller, Earl of Norfolk and Suffolk; Ralph his son, and Breton in-laws who rebelled against their Norman overlords. The name 'le Roos' appears in 1382 when Sir Thomas Roos owned Wissett Manor.

By the time of the Civil War and the Commonwealth, Charles Fleetwood is Lord of the Manor of Wissett and le Roos. In 1652 this Major General Fleetwood married Bridget, the widowed daughter of Cromwell; but the couple lived in Buckinghamshire. Wissett Lodge is named in the *Commonwealth Domesday* survey as being in ruins! Presumably by the 1660s it was well enough renovated, for it was the steward's house for the Fleetwoods of Chediston Hall (the seat of George Fleetwood, brother to Charles).

3. The third manorial tradition can be linked in here, since Chediston Hall had previously been held in the lordship of the Norton dynasty, that had owned the sub-manor of Wissett known as Blenche's (after Henry Blenche the owner in 1275).

By the time of the 1839-41 Tithe record, Sir William Edmund C Hartopp, Bart., is listed as 'the owner of a farm in the said Parish called the Lodge Farm, containing, by estimation, Four Hundred and Thirty-four Acres and Twenty nine Perches, and in the occupation of Mr John Tillott.' Hartopp, descended from the Fleetwoods via the female line, died in 1864, and a private act of parliament was required for the family to sell the estate.

Thus it was that in 1875 a new person owned Wissett Lodge, Frederick Charsley. But by the early 1890s, yet another family took over: Geoffrey Fynes Hollway was at The Lodge, while the title Lord of the Manor was conferred on Henry Calthrop Hollway-Calthrop Esq, of Stanhoe, near King's Lynn.

In the early 1900s, Annie Oxborough, as a young woman in service at The Lodge, would sometimes eulogize her 'immensely rich' employers, now 'Pozzo' ('Pots o' Money'), now 'the Ewbanks,' who, it was hinted, made their name in carpet-sweepers. Annie lived in, sleeping in a little back room at the top of the narrow spiral stairs, where she'd convince herself she could hear the 'rustle of silk' from the ghostly lady who was supposed to haunt the place. Some time before World War I Miss Florence Rebecca Ewbank acquired Wissett Lodge. Upon her death in June 1915, The Lodge was entrusted to her executor, Major Bartle Grant, a distant connection. Since the Major's son, Duncan, and his pacifist friends were desperately seeking to avoid being called up to fight in the Great War, it was decided that if they could prove they were doing some useful alternative labour, they would stand a better chance before the Ipswich Tribunal of 'perfectly bovine country bumpkins.'

*Wissett Lodge.*

So from the privileged salons of Bloomsbury, they came to Wissett Lodge, to be farmers.

This was the year 1916. The 'Bloomsbury set' of London intellectuals all traipsed up to Wissett Lodge, headed by Duncan Grant and Vanessa Bell who both painted, and David 'Bunny' Garnett. Duncan was the lover of both the others. When they weren't painting murals onto the venerable walls, or tipping their white leghorn hens' tails blue, they pretended to be horses ploughing a field. The part of the estate they had to cultivate was a mere six acres, but the fragile Vanessa and her even more fragile sister, Virginia Woolf, could not cope with the apple orchards and diseased blackcurrant bushes.

Throughout that spring and summer, a number of 'Bloomsberries' - who 'loved in triangles and lived in squares,' came to visit Vanessa, Duncan and Bunny. Lytton Strachey, the 'bearded stick-insect,' balked at the overgrown vegetation and 'thistles four feet high'; the exotic Lady Ottoline Morrell tried to be tolerant, writing afterwards in her journal:

> ' .....perhaps untidiness with sunshine wouldn't matter. It is dampness that makes it dark and depressing – But I loved the people – and enjoyed most awfully being there.'

Little did she realize that Vanessa was also writing afterwards, 'We're recovering from Ott, whose visit nearly destroyed us.' Virginia Woolf, inspired by the quietude of the place, arrived at the initial idea for her novel *Night and Day*, according to Frances Spalding, Vanessa Bell's biographer.

The Bloomsbury idyll of Wissett came to an abrupt end when the Central Tribunal announced that Duncan and Bunny could no longer pose as self-employed farmers. So once they had scrubbed the hectic murals off the walls (at the command of Duncan's disgusted father) they upped and went.

Local people can distantly remember their grandparents talking about 'poetry in the summerhouse at the back of Ives' in Bridge Street, Halesworth. Amongst the local poets, the 'Bloomsberries' too would read their work there.

The between-war years at The Lodge have become rather hazy. A lady who was a maid when Wissett Lodge was in the hands of Mr Barnard and Mr Slater served tea every so often to those two gentlemen, 'who popped up to The Lodge in their plus-fours to survey the fields and animals.' Mr Barnard was a fishing fleet owner, and Mr Slater, thin and moustachioed, was a cattle-drover. His wife, Mrs Annie Patience Slater, is remembered much more recently by Joan Meek as her grandmother, and mother of her own mother, Margaret Meek of Whitehouse Farm. It is said that Mr Harry Walker hired The Lodge from Barnard and Slater. Harry went to the USA, where he met his wife Mabel. Elizabeth Davey remembers that when she was a girl, she used to accompany Creamy Frost the milkman in his cart to deliver milk at The Lodge. Mabel used to give her chocolates, and when Elizabeth had gone away to work, Mabel asked Mr Frost what happened to 'that nice little girl. Ask her back here next time she's home.' Elizabeth continues: 'It must have been about 1935; I was a teenager then. She asked me if I'd be her lady's maid. I had to wash her, because she was partially paralyzed. They moved to Dennington Hall, and Harold Cutts, who was their chauffeur, and I moved with them. I drove round in their big Hillman. When the war came, they had to go to America.'

The war years saw some excitement at The Lodge, in the two evacuees from Dagenham - John and Derek Noble - and the crash of the British Lancaster bomber on 20 December 1943, in the field known as Hurren's Field two hundred yards south east of Lodge Farm. Six of the seven crew survived. There was a great deal of debris over a wide area - mainly broken windows, fallen ceilings and dislodged tiles. Sunny Whatling and his sister guarded the pilot, Flying Officer Don Field, until help arrived from Lodge Cottage. During the war, there were new people managing Wissett Lodge: the Fletchers and then the Longquests. The Kiddy family arrived from Withersfield, near Haverhill, in 1954: Albert and Dorothy Kiddy and their two sons, David and Gerald. Gerald and his bride, Margaret, started their life in Wissett together in one of the Lodge Cottages. The Kiddys have done an enormous amount for the village, its church, and its history. Margaret was responsible for overseeing the intricate embroidery of the new hassocks in the church. When Albert and Dorothy retired to their new bungalow, Rickyards, Gerald and Margaret took on the management of The Lodge where they had moved with their children, Geoffrey and Deborah. Geoffrey later married Claire Brinton, and after a spell in No 2 Lodge Cottage, they took over The Lodge on Margaret and Gerald's retirement. Their children are: Edward (7), Emily (5) and Henry (3). As well as running the farm, they are very active within the parish. Claire is not only president of the local Women's Institute, and a devoted co-founder and organizer of the children's Spiders' Club, but she is renowned for her cuisine at social gatherings. Both she and Geoffrey are on various parish and council committees. Geoffrey is chairman of the Parish Council, and treasurer for the Parochial Church Council.

## Lodge Barn

This used to be a cart-shed by the milking yard that belonged to Wissett Lodge on the great Hartopp estate.

It was converted by the Kiddys into a dwelling house in the latter part of the twentieth century. The first to live here were Mr and Mrs Wright, who ran Edward's the clothes shop in Halesworth. They were succeeded by Ken Gibson and his wife Barbara, an enthusiastic contributor to the W I movement.

It is rumoured that two people, on separate occasions, drowned in The Lodge pond (the one painted by Vanessa Bell in 1916) opposite Lodge Barn, and that at times you can hear the 'rustle of silk' as a phantom lady comes out of the barn and wafts straight across the pond. She was 'seen' one moonlit night by Mr Mann, who worked at The Lodge and lived at Hill House before Lizzie Eagle Bott. His ghostly sightings were the talk of the village for weeks.

The present owner is Alexander (George) Apthorpe, a writer, whose parents owned Fairstead Farm that used to be part of the Manor of Wissett and was famed country-wide for its October Bullock Fairs.

## Rydal Mount

This residence was built in the 1890s. Ann and Len Griffiths who lived here until recently had a strange requirement entailed in their deeds: to pay 12s 6d to a person in Boston, Massachusetts, via the NatWest Bank. Some say that the place was built for the first owner's mistress, which might account for the mysterious 12s 6d that would pay for the upkeep of the mistress and any issue.

In the 1925 Kelly's Directory, William K Campbell is listed as a private resident, and Robert William K Campbell his successor by 1933. The Campbells stayed through the first few years of the war. The Sadd family apparently were in service there in the 1940s. The 1945 electoral register notes that Edwin, Ernest, and Julia Sadd were living at Rydal Mount. Thereafter it became the refuge of a Pole whose family had been murdered in the war. This 'Major Buchowski' flew his Polish flag from Rydal Mount rooftop on Polish National Day. According to local hearsay, he married a Scots girl who played tennis and whose father had been a governor in the Sudan.

During the war, the German bombers flying in over Southwold and Holton (using the windmill to get their bearings before heading south to London, guided by the Halesworth-Liverpool Street railway) frequently discharged bombs on anything moving below. One plane dropped two landmines by Rydal Mount. The blast shredded all Mrs Campbell's stockings to bits, the tale goes. Everyone was so covered in soot as they ran down to the village alerting their neighbours that they were unrecognizable.

Ann and Len, who bought Rydal Mount in 1978 from Norman ('played tennis for England') and Daisy Giles, recount several stories about their friendly ghost, who opens and shuts doors. She's a nun-like lady, dressed all in grey, and has been seen by Ann and Len's daughter, Lesley. Moreover, Len's mother, knowing nothing about the ghost, said to Ann one day, 'I think there's a ghost in Lesley's room: she's standing at the end of the bed.'

The new owners of Rydal Mount are Kathleen and Alan Witherby, whose publishing house, Witherby International Publishing, specializes in shipping and insurance.

*Publishers colophons from the house of Witherby:*
*1. HF & G Witherby. Alan Witherby's grandfather*
*HF Witherby, a well-known ornithologist,*
*published bird-books.*

*2. Witherby International Publishing.*
*Alan publishes, and his wife Kathleen edits.*

*Beverley Nichols as a child at The Red House, 1903.*

## The Red House

In the 1830s, this stately red brick mansion was owned by Robert Tacon and run, along with other Wissett estates, by Richard Allen. By the 1850s, Robert's son, Richard Tacon, was farming at The Red House and by 1869 was recorded as 'landowner.' The 1881 census enters Richard as eighty years old, and farming a hundred acres (presumably including other farms) with four men and a boy. His housekeeper was Lucy Jackson, and his servant, George Boatman. By 1892 Edward Bean had taken over the management.

In 1902 John Nichols, a Bristol Conservative councillor, bought the property from Charles Tacon, Richard's son. The Red House is described as 'a rambling place with fifty-four acres of land.' Of John and Pauline Nichols' three sons, John Beverley, the baby, grew up to become the well-known writer, Beverley Nichols. He 'remembered Wissett with happy affection,' recalling 'idyllic summer days .......exploring the richly beautiful countryside, and cold, hard winters crouching in front of a blazing fire toasting muffins for tea.'

John Nichols senior left Wissett as suddenly as he had arrived, selling to Colonel Harry Lake in 1904. Harry Lake's daughter, Molly, who was then a girl of five, grew up to become a celebrated ballerina, who danced with Pavlova and Markova. Her diary is full of high spirits, whether about escapades with Freddie the head groom; or her brother Peter being chased naked through the village after falling into a pond; or cheeky encounters with the village schoolmaster.

The fiery Colonel Lake also owned Wissett Grange (qv). Molly trained at famous dance establishments, and later, with her husband Travis Kemp, set up exciting new ballet companies, particularly the Conservatoire in Ankara, Turkey. Travis' niece, Vicky Kemp, remembers 'Auntie Molly' with affection.

In 1919 Colonel Lake sold to Captain Harry Walker Eastcott. There exists a 1925 Notice For Sale for Captain Eastcott 'who is leaving the county.' The reason for his leaving was believed to have been the arrival of Mr Henry F Forbes as Mrs Ida Mary Eastcott's companion. In the church, on the chancel lectern, is a beautiful black leather-bound *Book of Common Prayer*, inscribed 'To the Glory of God - presented to Wissett Parish Church by H Eastcott, J.P., Gateshead-on-Tyne, January 1925.'

119

Mrs Dora Warren remembers working for the Eastcotts during the Second World War. One of her daily tasks was to take three churns of milk to the Halesworth Dairy (pre-Wagg) on a cart drawn by Hazel the mare. On one occasion, she was shot at by a German bomber overhead; the bullet went skeetering between Dora and the green camouflaged van ahead, which was probably the target as it was thought to be carrying military equipment.

Miss Doris Eastcott, the elder daughter, moved to a bungalow on the Westhall road. She must have been passionate about spring bulbs, because she was seen lifting (legally and with permission, by all accounts ) all the bulbs out of one side of Mill Cottage, up Mill Road. When Mrs Daphne Ritchie moved in to that cottage, the east side of the garden was noticeably depleted!

The Red House had quarters that were let out to Dr Dickson and family, who were friendly with the Meeks at Whitehouse Farm, and the Wetmores of Church Cottages, where they also stayed at one time.

The day that the present owners of the estate, the Tomkins, moved in (4 February 1963) caused quite a stir. Lieutenant Colonel Mike Tomkin tells the manner of their arrival:

'It was the coldest winter I can remember. Snow and ice everywhere. We had spent four nights at The Angel, Halesworth, before setting out for Wissett with two horses, a pony, five geese and three children. I knew I'd never get up Gray's Lane with the trailer, so I decided to come the back way over the Wash. I still got stuck - by Bleach Farm. By chance, John Hammond (related to Roy of Pear Tree Farm) suddenly appeared with a tractor and snow plough. I told him I'd unload the horses and walk with them if John would tug the car, which he did.'

What with that, and the excitement of Rex, the seventeen-hand hunter, escaping round the village, eventually they all made it safely to The Red House. Patricia Willis remembers that as a schoolgirl she was in such awe of Rex that she could never have

*Farming at Red House Farm, early 1900s.*

*Lieutenant Colonel
Mike Tomkin.*

imagined she would be exercising him regularly for Mike a few years on.

Occasionally Patricia and Rex would encounter the Tomkin boys, Alastair and Richard, zooming around in their car, learning to drive. They hadn't got to the road stage yet. Patricia remembers Caroline, the boys' sister, whose pony Patricia used to exercise before handling Rex.

Both Mike and his wife Peggy are from distinguished Suffolk families and since coming to Wissett have devoted their lives to the local community as well as to the county. Peggy, descended from the eminent Bunburys, was an ATS in the war, driving an ambulance ('and boring old generals') and also a 'FANY' (First Aid Nursing Yeomanry). She served on the magistrates bench in Halesworth, Framlingham and Saxmundham, and was a divisional commissioner for the NE Suffolk Guides. Peggy's nephew, Sir Michael Bunbury, will be President Elect of the Suffolk Show in 2002.

Mike Tomkin followed in his father's tradition of being High Sheriff of Suffolk for a year. When Mike and his brother were lads in West Suffolk, they used to be taken by a friend's father on train-rides via Halesworth to Southwold, to go fishing off Southwold pier. The platform at Halesworth formed the level crossing on the Old Norwich Road. What used to enthral the boys was that the platform was moveable: it was swung out in two halves over the road, then swung back to form two platforms either side of the road as the train approached. Mike remembers that his friend's father always had a box of worms dispatched from Felixstowe to Halesworth Station, where they'd pick it up en route for their fishing expedition.

During the war, Mike served in the 5th Royal Inniskilling Dragoon Guards, and was awarded the Military Cross in 1942 after the Battle of Alamein. In the 1960s, Mike was on the Wainford Rural District Council, and thereafter a county councillor for Halesworth, Deputy Lieutenant of Suffolk, High Sheriff of Suffolk, Chair of Suffolk Police Authority, and, in 1984, President of Suffolk Show.

Within Wissett, Mike was responsible, in 1970, for taking over the administration of the village hall from the church, and was chairman of the Village Hall Committee for a great many years. Among many other donations to the community, he gave the three flags: St Andrew's, St George's, and the Union Jack.

## Red House Bungalow

Lieutenant Colonel and Mrs Tomkin of The Red House had this bungalow built for their gardener/housekeeper couple in the late 1960s.

Sheila and Denis Pepper were there for seventeen years, before Marina and Richard Collison moved from Gisleham to take over from the Peppers. The Collisons were splendid gardeners, and transformed The Red House vegetable garden. They have many prize-winning shields from local horticultural shows. They moved in 1997, though Marina still works part-time in Wissett, for the Burtons at Wissett Grange. Gill and William Wright moved into Red House Bungalow for a brief spell, to be followed by the present occupiers, Pam and Harold Wilding, who have come from Attleborough in Norfolk to work for the Tomkins.

## High House Farm

For as far back as people can remember, the Balls family have lived and farmed here. But in the nineteenth century, it was owned by the Tacons, and farmed by Richard Allen, who managed a number of other Wissett estates, such as Red House Farm and Corner Farm.

In the church is a big black leather-bound bible, inscribed by the Balls family in 'affectionate memory' of their parents, James Samuel (1888-1967) and Fanny Eliza Mary Balls (1888-1971) of High House Farm, Wissett.

Dora Warren, who was a land-girl on the farm during the war, remembers James Balls with affection, and Fanny as a 'dear, lovely woman.' Dora worked out on the fields with Geoffrey ('Bay,'for 'babe,' as he was the youngest son). One day a British plane flew overhead, dropping a green box which landed nearby. Dora and Bay rushed over to open it - but the contents were unmentionable! In summer, they used to go 'shocking', or stacking up the corn stooks. Dora would lead the horse and Bay followed with the plough.

He used to mutter anxiously, 'She'll have it on her feet in a minute,' meaning that she was walking very close to the horse's hooves. There were some hair-raising moments when bullets would be whizzing overhead. On one such occasion, Dora was ditching (cutting a ditch out ) on her own, when a bullet skimmed right by her into the hedge.

After her time with the Balls as a land-girl, Mr 'Tiger' Balls senior would hold her up as a paragon. 'Oh, she must have been a marvel,' said the subsequent land-girls. 'No she wasn't a marvel - she was a milliner!' retorted the old Mr Balls. The new land-girls kept wanting breaks and going to the lavatory. 'Tiger' senior would reprimand them with, 'The one who worked here before worked without a break and didn't have to leave the room once!' Dora was always amused by his calling the fields a 'room.' Mr Balls is remembered, by George Kerrison, for his booming voice which could be heard from several fields away.

# Halleluia

The age of this charming little cottage isn't known but is even more diminutive today than it was a hundred years ago. It had always been a farmworkers' cottage. The 1840 Tithe returns indicate it was owned by Robert Aldred of Whitehouse Farm.

Retired farmhands nowadays ruminate over a picturesque individual, a Mr Chapman, alias 'Pilfer.' He 'lived down Halleluia with his daughter Gutty, who used to push her little boy George round in his pram with a dummy' during the 1920s. Pilfer Chapman was well-known for his poaching prowess. He worked at Whitehouse Farm and previously at Bond's Farm too, for George Tyrrell, who was very fair to Pilfer and knew all about his peccadillos.

Arnold (Ernie) Read lived here as a young man. He was shepherd for Mr Godbold of Whitehouse Farm and people can still picture him leading the sheep 'up Buntkins' (Buntings Lane) and round to Halleluia. Another family, distantly recalled, is the Bakers. Geoff Baker worked for Mr Chute at Bulhams Covert.

In 1942 Stuart Meek purchased Whitehouse Farm along with Halleluia and in 1945 Emily and Thomas Pasfield were living here at the cottage. After them were Bill Hammond and his wife Phyllis (Ernie and Phyllis Read's daughter). In 1957 Jimmy and Helen Nunn moved here from Wissett Hall Cottage after Wissett Hall was sold, and they stayed here, 'hermit-like,' until 1964 when they moved to No 13 Brickhill Bungalows. Halleluia was then bought from Mr Meek by Colonel Tomkin of The Red House. The cottage had by that time stood empty for a decade at least. Richard Tomkin recalls an interesting interlude at Halleluia that happened in 1977, he thinks, while he was a student. His father, Mike, recounts that the well-known novelist Rose Tremain, who lived in Spexhall at the time, rang him up to ask if Halleluia could be used to film one scene of a play which she was writing for BBC Television. Mike agreed and later on that summer, at harvest time, the film was made: 'It was called *Halleluia: Mary Plumb - a short romance*. The scene in question was a fairly torrid love scene filmed in the rough ground behind the cottage. A surprisingly large BBC contingent and several vehicles including a canteen wagon appeared. It was a windy and sunny day with, at intervals, a lot of dust and noise caused by the Balls brothers' combine at work in the neighbouring field. This at times brought filming to a halt. At one point the girl's skirt was blown up over her knee and an attendant from the dresser's vehicle had to rush over and adjust it - something the actress could easily have done for herself. Anyway, the scene was completed satisfactorily.' The film was transmitted subsequently on 13 July 1980 on BBC Television, and Mike shared his £150 or so earnings with the Balls brothers.

In about 1983 the builders arrived and made the derelict Halleluia habitable again. Richard Tomkin moved in from The Red House soon after and is still there today. Richard has been very generous in providing use of land for major village events, such as the Treacle Fairs.

## Bleach Farm

This moated mill farm dates from about 1500. It was owned for at least three centuries by Alburgh Town Trust. Mr Reginald (Reggie) Elvin, who lived at the farm from 1954 to 1984, has copies of papers found in an old mouldy chest in Alburgh dating back to 1624, in the reign of James 1. These papers mention, among others, a Sir John Tasburgh and William Gooch in connection with lands and property in Wissett, as well as lands in Wortwell and various places along the Norfolk border.

By the time of the 1839-40 Tithe record, Bleach Farm was managed by James and Robert Aldred. From the field names listed then (Bleach Meadow, First Bleach, Second Bleach and Hempland) it is clear that hemp had been grown and processed there. James Aldred's father, in the 1780s, had a factory for hempen/linen cloth making in Halesworth, believed to have stood in Chediston street. James had a shop near the bridge in Halesworth; from here hemp was distributed through agents to a number of regions in Suffolk and Norfolk. James Aldred and his wife Sarah are both buried in Wissett churchyard. James died in 1846 aged sixty-seven, and Sarah, 'relict of James,' died in 1849, aged sixty-three.

Gerald Kiddy, following Arthur Young's work on agriculture in Suffolk in 1813, writes that Suffolk hemp was 'of a high quality and used for making table- and bed-linen, shirtings, etc.' It was the 'lower grade hemp imported from Russia' that was used for producing rope. Wissett Hemp was probably a dying industry even in Robert Aldred's day. The 1844 White's Directory for Wissett reports that 'great quantities of hemp were formerly grown in the neighbourhood and many of the inhabitants were employed in the Suffolk hempen cloth trade, but the trade was discontinued many years ago.' Gerald Kiddy thinks that it was probably killed off by competition from the Lancashire cotton mills.

The directories list William Catling as occupying Bleach Farm from the mid 1860s to the mid 1870s. After William and his wife Ellen (née Flaxman), John Tyrrell took over, as Mr Harry Buck recalls. John Tyrrell's brother was George Henry Tyrrell, soon to own Ash Tree Farm, and Harry Buck is George Tyrrell's grandson. The 1881 census states that John N Tyrrell from Westhall, who was twenty-four at the time, farmed twenty-four acres, employing three men. Apart from himself, his household consisted of his sixty-one-year-old mother and two young 'Farm Servants in Door' from Rumburgh: James Reynolds and James Cleveland.

From the 1890s to the end of the 1920s the Howlett family ran Bleach Farm: Thomas Howlett to about 1910, followed by James. In the 1930s, the Warren brothers worked at the farm, and carried on into the 1940s. Then Dora Taylor (daughter of Annie Oxborough) married one of the brothers, Alfred. The Warrens took in two evacuees from London: Jean and Vera Cockerton. Dora remembers one night, when she was on her own, being 'frightened by loud noises coming from above the bedroom ceiling which sounded like heavy chains being dragged to and fro across the attic floor.' Her husband investigated thoroughly the next day but found nothing disturbed and no sign of anything that would account for the noise. Dora and Alfred's daughter, Patricia (now Mrs Willis), was born here. After Alfred's death, Dora and Patricia went to stay awhile with Dora's mother.

In 1954, Reggie Elvin and his wife Beatrice took up the challenge of running the farm. It had fallen into disrepair, for the Alburgh Town Trust was not putting enough money into it to prevent major leaks and deterioration of the ancient beams of the farmhouse. Reggie and Beatrice can joke about it now, but the night they first moved in was far from funny. They were faced with fifteen sheets of tin on the roof, an outside WC, and the prospect of going to bed under an umbrella. Amongst the fallen roof slates in the garden, they found a four-thousand-year-old arrowhead and a millstone. Reggie locates the field known as Mill Mount to the south east of the moat, between Bonds Farm to the west, and Spexhall Manor to the east. He surmises that the mill itself stood at the top of a pathway leading down to the main road.

It took four years before Alburgh Town Trust allowed the Elvins to renovate the place, even though the sanitary inspectors instantly condemned it. 'There was a well 106 foot deep producing water not fit for the cows to drink,' says Reggie. He was able to instal a pump and storage tank, but repairing the farm took eight to ten years. At last Reggie bought the farm, cleaned out the moat, and continued to farm Friesian cattle, pigs and eighty-four acres of arable land. The Elvin's son, Derek, rode to Wissett school on a bike, quite a rare thing in the 1950s. He spent his teenage years at the farm. The thirty years that Reggie and Beatrice farmed at Bleach Farm were hard-going. Finally they sold up in 1984, and moved back to Stradbroke, where Reggie had been born. Reggie's greatest regret is that Bleach Farm has not been kept intact, but that different parts of it have been parcelled out and sold separately. Mr John Maynard at Spexhall Manor bought the farm and sold the farmhouse to Peter and Janet Ash, who were here for several years before selling in 1998. The present owners, Roy and Maureen Stoddard, from Clacton-on-Sea, are painstakingly restoring the farmhouse to its early seventeenth-century appearance. Peter Ash has kept the old barn which he is hoping to convert some time in the future.

## Willow Grange

In about 1899, this property was built for George Henry Bunbury, who had come from Ireland in the 1880s. In England, he had met and married the striking Harriet Eliza (Lily) Randall, granddaughter of the celebrated opera-singer, Eliza Invararity. George and Lily had five children: Vera, Ione, Cecil, Amy and Ralph. After the first two daughters were born, they went to Florida where George grew pineapples and planted orange and grapefruit trees. They returned to England for the birth of Cecil, then went back to Florida until the turn of the century. Eventually they sailed back to England and settled in Wissett, where George built Willow Grange, named after the battle (22-23 November 1899) in the Boer War. According to George's granddaughter, Patricia Stanford of Halesworth, her mother, Ione Bunbury, would have been ten or eleven then. Ione's name comes from the heroine of Lord Lytton's melodramtic romance, *The Last Days of Pompeii*, written in 1832-83. George and Lily's other children - Vera, Cecil, Amy and Ralph - also had particular associations, notably Cecil and Ralph. Cecil George St Pierre Bunbury was 'Cecil' after Cecil Rhodes, 'George' after his father, and as the elder son was 'St Pierre' according to his lineage from the house of St Pierre in Normandy under Henry de Boneberi. Ralph was 'Ralph Hereward,' after Hereward the Wake of the fens, whose rebellion was quashed by William the Conqueror in 1071.

Miss Stanford continues: 'Ralph was born at Willow Grange. He attended the Falkenberg School in Beccles as a day pupil. Cecil was a boarder at Framlingham

*Vera and Ione Bunbury in 1915.*

*George Henry Banbury*

College. The girls were educated at home by a governess.' The Bunburys stayed at The Grange until 1919 or 20. Ione married Wilfred Stanford (in 1922) who was brother to Joy, the owner of Ash Tree Farm with her husband Lewis Parry. Minnie Nunn, daughter of Sugar Nunn, had worked for Wilfred's parents in Halesworth, and once Wilfred was married, Minnie came to work for Wilfred's wife Ione. From her earnings, Minnie saved and saved until she had £24: just enough money to buy her first cow. This was to be the start of her three-acre smallholding at Laxfield, in which she crammed pigs, sheep, a few cows and her pony.

Little did George Henry Bunbury, descendant of the Irish branch of the family, imagine that, half a century later, the very next farmhouse along Gray's Lane, The Red House, would become home to a descendant of the English branch of Bunburys, Mrs Peggy Tomkin. Peggy's ancestor, Sir Charles Bunbury (1740-1821), did much to strengthen the prestige of the Jockey Club; it was his racehorse Diomed that was the winner of the first Derby in 1780.

By 1922 Willow Grange was in the ownership of a Mr Scott Shaw, whose time in Wissett nobody can remember. This was not the case with the next resident: Miss Gresy.

'Madame Cressy,' as she was known to the village girls in the late 1920s and 30s, always wore red and was thought to be French, perhaps because she and her mother bred French poodles and were driven by Bob Miller, their chauffeur, in a French car.

In 1945, according to the electoral register, a Pleasance G Foulcher was in residence at Willow Grange. Various families have lived at The Grange since the war, including Mr and Mrs Vic Gooch with their sons Michael and Peter, and Mr and Mrs Grove, the parents of Mrs Margaret Kiddy. The present owner is Lady Heygate.

## Peacehaven

This bungalow has been completely converted from old piggeries and stables that belonged to Captain Chute at Bulhams Covert. It was bought from the estate, after Captain Chute died, by Peter Fitch, who has done most of the modifications himself. Peter thinks that the piggeries were built in the late 1800s. He now lives there with Susan Smith and continues to improve the site. He has recently dug out the pond which had been filled in. Susan is a newly co-opted parish councillor, and works for Waveney District Council in the Conservation and Design Department.

## Peartree Farm *(previously listed as Peartree Villa, part of Pear Tree Farm)*

The rear wing of this five-bedroomed house dates from about 1640 and the front from about 1860. According to the 1840 Tithe record the farm - some sixty acres - was owned by Henry Bence Bence but occupied by James Goldsmith. James was a staunch non-conformist until he suffered dire misfortune, at which point his family received much solace from the Reverend Robert Kemp, so he switched to the Church of England.

The 1881 census reveals that 'Peartree Villa' was occupied by the labourer Henry Godfrey, his wife Hannah, their five young children, and Hannah's three older children by a previous marriage to a Mr Tovell. The next resident we know of is a Mrs Symonds who was here in 1894.

By 1900 Mr Harry Aldous was here. Harry had previously farmed at Bramfield and had also been the last miller at Halesworth. Harry and his wife Hannah (née Hurren) had three children: William (who married Emily Littlewood from Brook Hall Farm), Francis, and Elizabeth (Lizzie). Hannah had become an invalid after a fall and so Lizzie looked after the house, making butter, bread, beer and wine. At harvest, she would also help in the fields. When William's three children, Stanley, Violet and John, were of school age, their Auntie Lizzie would regularly take them down to Wissett school. Lizzie married George Kerrison, and gave birth to a son, also named George. Although they spent their later years with their son George in Scotland, both parents had expressed a wish to be buried in Wissett. When the time came, first George, in 1978, then Lizzie, in 1991, had to be conveyed by hearse down from the north to Wissett churchyard. Meanwhile, Lizzie's brother William had worked for his father-in-law at Brook Hall Farm after his own father had retired. John Aldous remembers being told that his Grandfather Harry hadn't been a well man, and so a wealthy relative in London had bought Pear Tree Farm for him thinking the fresh country air would improve his health. They would always keep the front room spare in case the wealthy relatives from London would come to visit. Local people say that much later, William became quite frail and committed suicide rather than go into a home.

Harry Aldous remained at Pear Tree Farm until at least 1929. Arthur Joseph Thurlow, associated with Laurel and Poplar Farms in Spexhall, had arrived at Pear Tree by 1933, while in 1936 or thereabouts Mr Lawrence Chute of Bulhams had bought the farm for his workers, and William and Rose Hammond were in residence. Their son Roy Hammond

*The annual outing of the congregational chapel Sunday School in c1905, with Harry Aldous at the horse's head.*

(of the Hammonds Garage business) has written some of his memories of his time here:

'I moved to Pear Tree Farm in 1936, when I was seven years old, with my parents and sister. The farm had been bought by Lawrence Chute and my father was farm manager. The farm had to be stocked with new equipment and Suffolk Punch horses. The latest thing on the market was known as "Morphreys", which was a tumbrel that could have a front section added to form a wagon at harvest time. After seven years a standard Fordson tractor was introduced to replace horses. This took an awful long time to get used to: it had a habit of not always starting and sometimes it would be 9 am before it was prepared to leave its shed.

'In the early part of the war, because we were living in a large house, my parents were asked to take in a family of evacuees from Dagenham, which was being heavily bombed. When the bus turned up with them, they were accompanied by the local School Nurse, commonly known as the "nit nurse." Their ages ranged from five to fourteen and they were totally confused because they had never seen the countryside or a live farm animal. I remember we were all very concerned when the nurse said that they were not to enter the house, due to the fact that they were accompanied by fleas and lice, and their hair was full of nits. We all felt so sorry for them because the nurse insisted on shaving their heads. This was not so bad for the younger children but the older (13-14 year old) girls who had lovely long hair had to be caught and held by my father whilst their heads were also shaved. Their clothes had to be burnt and they had to be bathed; it appears that they had never had a proper bath before. I think they were with us for one or two years and were

129

treated as part of the family, and mother took pride in having all eight children turned out clean and smart for school each morning.'

'Whilst they were with us, two landmines dropped nearby, one near Rydal Mount and one in a field away from our house. These caused tremendous damage to the house but fortunately, apart from for a few cuts, no-one was hurt. This happened late evening when dark and my sister (five years younger than me) was in bed upstairs. All the evacuees were in the downstairs bedroom and were quickly accounted for. Due to general confusion, ceiling down etc., it was an effort for my parents to get upstairs to my sister's room but when they got there they found the ceiling suspended over the bed and my sister still asleep underneath, unharmed. This was when the evacuees were taken away and temporary repairs carried out to our house and I continued to live there, apart from National Service, until I got married.

'I attended Wissett School when we moved to Pear tree Farm, having started at Rumburgh School. Wissett School had a very small number of local children. When evacuees arrived in the area, two extra classes were added and included a male teacher, brought in from London. He was very liberal with the cane which we had not experienced before. Between 1936 and the war, we were given a treat about every six weeks by Mr Miller, who I think was a fishing skipper. Whenever he arrived home after a fishing trip he would come to the school and give us a pennyworth of sweets.

'At the age of ten, I attended Halesworth Edgar Sewter School. We were not allowed to go to school if the air raid siren had gone off before we arrived. This was a very regular occurrence for a period of time and was taken advantage of by a large number of pupils, who intended to arrive late hoping the siren would go off before they arrived. Having got to school, an awful lot of time was spent in the air raid shelter, built on the north boundary of the school. Once, during the lunch break, we noticed a huge fire in the Chediston direction and a large number of us decided to take off and investigate. It turned out that the army had moved out of Chediston Hall that day and set fire to a lot of documents in the fireplaces, which set fire to the chimney and the rest of the building. Due to the number of children not at school, the Headmaster called in the dreaded Local Attendance Officer to collect the children and get them back to school. He spent the afternoon chasing us in his Austin Seven around the parkland with little success, as there was a lot of woodland and plenty of hiding places. This was reported to my parents, who decided that I would be better off at a different school and I finished my education at Ilketshall St Lawrence, under an excellent Headmaster, Mr Wurr. Mr Wurr not only did a good job at school, but also made sure you got the correct rate of pay and working conditions for some years after leaving school.

'During the war years, if you were classed as a "Strong Boy," a farm could apply to have you help on the farm and this I did for several years, for weeks at a time. Due to strict rationing, food of course was a priority during these years, and at a very early age, probably eleven, I learnt to shoot rabbits, hares, partridges and occasionally pheasants. Mother would turn these into mouth-watering dishes and if I was able to get more than required there was a ready market, as people were really short of food; even rooks could be sold at a local butcher.

'One spring evening, during the war, I was walking west up a long meadow, at the bottom of the hill below Pear Tree Farm. It was a very still evening and suddenly, for no reason whatsoever, I saw the trees at the end of the meadow blow over as they would in a gale of wind. I also noticed the tall grass being flattened in front of me. It suddenly hit me, almost blowing me over and was followed by a tremendous explosion. This was caused by the bomb dump at Metfield Airfield blowing up and, unfortunately, there were a lot of American lives lost. This caused a tremendous amount of damage to the Metfield area and even blew windows out and roof tiles off Pear tree Farmhouse at that distance.

'I left school at fourteen years of age, and started work at a garage in Halesworth as an apprentice. I was taken on at 7s 6d (37p) a week for 48 hours. However, after two weeks I was offered 10s (50p) provided I worked until 6 pm on Saturday afternoons. This I gladly did. Because of food rationing, it was difficult to provide packed lunches, so most of the time I would bike to work for 8 am, home to lunch and back again all within an hour, and possibly back to Halesworth in the evening for recreational purposes, particularly on Saturday evenings when the local cinema was a must. Cowboy films were very popular, also war films such as *The Dambusters* were always packed out. I think these were produced and marketed as morale boosters.

'I was called up at eighteen, for two years and I served in Malta and the Middle East. I married a Halesworth girl in 1953 and moved to Halesworth. My parents are both buried in Wissett Churchyard.'

After the Hammonds were a Mr and Mrs Pietrzak and their children. Mr Pietrzak lived here but farmed at Withersdale. The next newcomers to Peartree were Paul and Penny Lucas with their three children. Paul ran his business from the house employing seven people at one time. His business was building small-scale models of building complexes. They built the Castle Mall in Norwich to scale six times. They have modelled developments from the Shetlands to St Helier in Jersey, from Swansea to Norwich and in the South of France. The company outgrew Peartree Villa, so the business relocated to Little Beck, and the Lucases went to live in Bungay. Sadly Paul died recently after a long illness. He kept in touch with Wissett and his presence on busking nights at The Plough will always be remembered.

The present owners, Ann and Gale Sieveking, are both archaeologists. Gale's interests stretch from the Far East, where he conducted excavations in Malaysia, Thailand and Australia and, most locally, Grimes Graves in the Norfolk Breckland and High Lodge, Mildenhall, in Suffolk. In the 1960s and 70s he excavated both of these sites for the British Museum, where he worked for most of his career. Ann's field of research is palaeolithic art, ranging from the painted and engraved caves of Western Europe to the miniature decorated objects of this period found all over the Europe and as far afield as Central Asia. She has published a number of books and articles on this subject.

*Denis Watson, Mr Blowers, Mr and Mrs Chute with their daughter-in-law and Mary Reeder at Bulhams.*

# Bulhams Covert

The origins of Bulhams as a farmstead is hard to determine as on the 1840 Tithe map there is no house marked, although there is evidence of some previous community here. The packway that goes past Bulhams and out on to the Wissett/Rumburgh road near the old entrance to Valley Farm was used by drovers taking their animals to the ancient fairs, particularly the Bullock Fair which was held at Fairstead Farm. The main landowners around Bulhams were Henry Bence Bence and Robert Tacon. Bulhams Covert ('Wood') itself was owned by Tacon, but individual strip fields surrounding the covert, many with 'Bulhams' in their name, belonged not just to Bence and Tacon, but to various people such as Mary Forster, Thomas Ling and Thomas Garrod. A number of Tacon's fields had 'Spatchet' in their name, suggesting their use for 'spatching' or 'dispatching' game birds.

There was a double dwelling at 'Bullens Covert' by 1881, as the census for that year shows that John Boatman, an agricultural labourer aged sixty-five, and his son Frederick, aged twelve, lived in one side; and in the other: Mary Ann Muttitt, a widow of sixty-four, her two sons in their twenties, Robert and William, and her nineteen-year-old daughter Martha.

The modern Ordinance Survey map indicates both a Bulhams Farm and a Bulhams Covert. Clearly there was a farm by 1908; a Harry Pearce is recorded in that year as farm bailiff to Jabez Paine Esq, of Bulhams Farm. By 1916, George Paine had taken on the role of farm bailiff to Jabez. A memorandum of 29 July 1919 records the sale of Bulhams, a 'Compact Small Farm,' by George Paine, vendor, to Lawrence Vere Chute, purchaser. Interestingly, this document shows that the wife of the writer Henry Rider Haggard had managed a two-acre 'piece or parcel' of land known as 'Bulham' for some years previously.

Lawrence Vere Chute MC was installed by 1922 at Bulhams, which he is believed to have acquired with the proceeds from the sale of a stamp collection. The Chutes were related to Chaloner William Chute of 'The Vyne,' Sherborne St John, Hampshire, which is now a National Trust stately home. Mr Lawrence Chute is remembered as being wheelchair-bound in his old age. He died in 1948, four years after his wife Nora. Both are buried in Wissett churchyard. The running of the farm was taken over by their son Antony Vere Chute after the Second World War. Captain Antony (Tony) Chute was in the Royal Artillery during the war, and was captured in the Western Desert in 1941 - 42. He spent the rest of the war as a prisoner. Daphne, his wife, was in the ATS (Auxiliary Territorial Service). They had three sons: Robin, Chaloner and Richard.

Tony started a successful Elite Hybrid Pig Breeding unit. He was also a magistrate of the Blything Bench and chairman of the Parish Council for some years. He and his wife were both keen tennis players and Daphne is remembered for her afternoon tea parties. Colonel Tomkin recalls that she was the only person he knew that put out name place cards for these tea parties. Daphne did a great deal of charity work and is remembered, before she became ill from cancer, as regularly driving people to and from hospital for appointments. The Chutes employed several men to help with the working of the farm and had already before the war bought Pear Tree Farm and house for their farm manager William Hammond to live in. Daphne and Tony died within a few years of each other and their son Robin sold the land to Mr Percy Hadingham. The house was rented out for several years to Mr and Mrs Pye-Watson and others, before it was bought in 1995 by John and Brenda Kemp. They came from Shadingfield with their daughters Sarah and Rachel and Brenda's mother Barbara Leggett.

## Brook Hall Farm

This old farmhouse is listed as a '16C building which stands on the remains of a large irregularly moated site.'

Back in 1327, a Petro del Broke (Peter of the Brook) being the freeholder of Brokes, Brokes Hall or Brookes Hall, paid 4s 4d in tax, so we believe it is where the name Brook Hall comes from. There have been many owners and occupiers since then but the Garolde/Garrould family owned it for about two hundred years between the sixteenth and eighteenth century. In 1824 it was bricked over and the roof tiled, with the result that the clay and beamed walls and thatched roof were covered up. It was also extended both ends. The moat would have originally gone completely round the house but it has been filled in to make way for the farm buildings. It is a working farm which has remained much the same acreage for many years. It is thought that at one time Brook Hall could have guarded the north end of a Manor Deer Park. In 1830 a probate was granted on the will of Robert Balls, who was then the owner of Brookes Hall, and he left the farm to his daughter Martha and her husband John Button.

*Brook Hall Bees.*

In 1855 the farm was sold to Jonathan Howlett (the auctioneer of Wissett Hall) then aged fifty-four. In 1869 there was an Edward Rush farming here for Jonathan Howlett, followed in the 1870s by William Dunnett. According to the 1881 census, Benjamin Howlett was farm bailiff for Jonathan, living here with his young wife Fanny, and employing nine men and two boys. By 1888, Jonathan Howlett had died and the executors had put his 730 acres (which included Brook Hall and Wissett Hall) up for auction. It was bought by the Durrant family but by 1920 it had changed hands again. James Flaxman Littlewood was in possession and by 1927 his son George Robert Littlewood had taken over. James and his wife Emily retired to No 5 The Street (The Homestead). During George's time here, a builder, Fred Bowers (whose brother worked at The Swan Inn) was in the act of repairing one of the many wells when he was overcome by fumes and died. Before this untimely moment, however, Mr Bowers had helped to build the Wissett Lodge cottages and repair The Lodge itself.

In 1944 Mr Henry Duncan came from working in the fish market in Liverpool to try his luck at farming. His son, Alan, thought it was a brave move as his father had lost a leg in the First World War and had no experience of farming other than keeping a few chickens and bees in the back garden in Liverpool. The main farm enterprise then at Brook Hall was poultry. There were twenty thousand birds, the majority being poussins. The bees did very well too and a large amount of honey was sold to Fortnum and Masons. One beehive produced over two hundred pounds of honey. They had about seventy-five hives and advertised for the location of swarms at 7s 6d a hive. One Sunday morning, on the ringing of the church bells, they got twelve swarms!

Mr Duncan left in 1949 and was succeeded by Mr Jacob Bakus, who started the dairy unit. The dairy was continued by George Flaxman when he bought the estate in 1955. George and his wife Phyllis had previously farmed at St Peter South Elmham. They had six children: Doug, Jean, Joy, Ian, Colin and Jill. Brook Hall remained a dairy farm until 1966 when the cows were sold and a pig fattening unit was set up. By this time, the four older children had left home and Colin was helping his father. The farm has changed from reliance on the farmer and six men using horsepower alone in the early 1900s to being completely mechanized at the beginning of the twenty-first century. Jill Flaxman, the last child, married an 'Aussie,' Stuart Smith, in 1979 and moved to Australia to live. At the wedding, Colin Flaxman met Stuart's sister Helen and they married a year later, in 1980!

George and Phyllis then moved to Beccles and Colin and Helen have farmed Brook Hall to the present day. They have four children: Emma (19), Nicholas(17), Edward(15) and Andrew(11).

## Brook Hall Cottage

This cottage was built as two tenements for the farmworkers at Brook Hall Farm, we think, in the late seventeenth or early eighteenth century. On the 1839 Wissett Tithe map, it is listed as being owned, along with the farm, by Mr John Button .

When George Littlewood had Brook Hall Farm between 1927 and 1944, there were two families living in the cottage, the Pages and the Gillingwaters. Apparently the Gillingwaters had eleven children, which must have made the walls bulge somewhat!

In 1945 Leonard and Violet Baker and Stanley and Alice Goward were there. Jimmy Andrews, and then Mr Doughty, were the last ones to be living in the cottage and working for the owner of the farm, since farms were becoming increasingly mechanized. The cottage fell into disrepair and was sold away from the farm by George Flaxman to Mr John Kingham, a builder from Kent, in 1966. Mr Kingham renovated it and rented it out - at one stage to the singer Cat Stevens and his backing band. Colin Flaxman, whose father owned Brook Hall then, recalls hearing the music floating across the fields.

Mr Stuart Burt, an ex-army helicopter pilot, occupied the place for several years, then Mrs Sandeman-Allen, followed by Mr and Mrs Wolf, and then in 1981 Ron and Dinah Bridle. The Bridles did a fair amount of work on the building, including extensions to both ends. Sadly Ron died in 1998 and Dinah moved to Southwold, selling to the present owners, Jim and Pauline Hayward, from Holton, who run the second-hand bookshop in Halesworth.

# The Yokel's Memories

1   *Silly Suffick we are called*
*But dew yew know the reason why?*
*Thas not cos we are fuelish*
*As that fare ter signify*

2   *Silly stem from saelig*
*A war'd from Anglo-Saxon days*
*What mean that we are blessed*
*And hev pure an Holy ways*

3   *Oi wus bred an' born in Suffick*
*On a farm far out 'a 'reach*
*Oive never travelled very far*
*So imparfick is moi speech*

4   *Sum folks hully loike ter roam*
*An travel far an' wide*
*But oive allus got moi pleasures*
*From the Suffick countryside*

5   *Oive lived a 'long a nature*
*Unner Suffick's fickle sky*
*An sumtoimes thow't the march*
   *of toime*
*Hed allmus parst me by*

6   *The blagbud an' the mavish sung*
*Dune ivery lane an' loke*
*An' in the thicket could be hard*
*The "tupp" "tupp" of the pudden-e-poke*

7   *Oi recollect at haysel toime*
*Fourses neath the trees*
*An moi corduroys kipt orf moi boots*
*By the fillus tied under moi knees*

8   *When the owd cock crew on a*
   *harvest morn*
*Oi'd spuffle out abroad*
*And riddy clunk moi sickle bler'd*
*As keen as a viking sword*

9   *Oi ploughed the furra's straight an deep*
*As oi tarned the rich dark sile*
*With the clop, clop of the hosses hoofs*
*Oi walked the slubby mile*

10  *Himsumiver toimes hev changed*
*An' for the warst oi fear*
*Toime don't fer to larst as long*
*As it did in yisteryear.*

One of a series of poems in Suffolk dialect by Elizabeth Davey.

# Short Bibliography

Anglo-Saxon Chronicle:  Edited GN Garmonsway (Dent 1955)

Barrett, Hugh:  Early To Rise: A Suffolk Morning
    (Faber & Faber 1967)
  A Good Living (Old Pond 2000)

Bell, Adrian:  Men and the Fields (Batsford 1939)
  The Flower and the Wheel (Bodley Head 1949)

Benari, Naomi:  Vagabonds and Strolling Players (printed by
    Avon Lithe Ltd, under the Auspices of
    Imperial Society of Teachers on dancing)

Connon, Bryan:  Beverley Nichols: A Life (Constable 1991)

Dymond, David,  An Historical Atlas of Suffolk (Suffolk County
  & Martin, Edward:  Council & Suffolk Institute of Archaeology
    and History 3rd edition 1999)

Eagle Bott, Elizabeth:  I Looked Over the Gate (Ipswich Book Co, Nacton)

Ewart Evans, George:  Where Beards Wag All (Faber & Faber 1971)
    "    "    "

  & Gladwell, David:  Requiem for the Village (filmscript 1973)

Flint, Brian:  Windmills of East Anglia (FW Pawsey 1971)

Fordham, Mike:  The Agricultural Labourer 1720 - 1900
    (Adshop, Halesworth)

Ingate, Mary:  The Sound of the Weir (Macmillan 1977)

James, PD:  Cover Her Face  (Sphere Books)
  "  "  Unnatural Causes (  "    "  )

Kiddy, Margaret:  St Andrew's, Wissett: A Guide (KDS reprinted 1997)

Kinsey, Gordon:  Pulham Pigs (Terence Dalton Ltd,
    Lavenham, Suffolk 1988)

Lytton, Lord:  The Last Days of Pompeii (Routledge 1834)

Mee, Arthur:  Suffolk (Hodder & Stoughton 1951)

Munro Cautley, H:  Suffolk Churches (Norman Allard 3rd edition 1954)

Newby, James:  Independency in Halesworth and District
    (WE Fairweather, Halesworth 1936)

Nichols, Beverley:  A Case of Human Bondage (1966)

Scarfe, Norman:  Suffolk - A Shell Guide (Faber & Faber 1960)

Seymour, Miranda:  Ottoline Morrell: Life on the Grand Scale

Sieveking, Ann:           The Cave Artists (Thames & Hudson)
Sieveking, Ann and Gale: The Caves of France and Northern Spain (Vista Books)
Spalding, Frances:        Paper Darts (Collins & Brown 1991)
Sparkes, Ivan:           Halesworth Through the Ages, Vols 1-7
                          (Adshop, Halesworth)
Suffolk Domesday:        Edited by Alex Rumble ( Phillimore 1986)
Woolf, Virginia:         Night and Day (Penguin 1969)

*A flight over Wissett with Ernie Woolnough in his microlite.*